PEACEABLE KINGDOM

Michigan Artists Reply to Edward Hicks

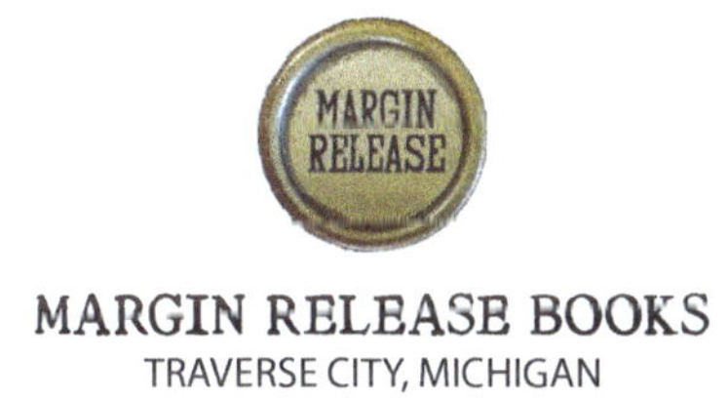

MARGIN RELEASE BOOKS
TRAVERSE CITY, MICHIGAN

PEACEABLE KINGDOM

MICHIGAN ARTISTS
REPLY TO EDWARD HICKS

Edited by
Daniel Stewart

michigan artists gallery
317 E. Front Street
Traverse City, MI 49684
michiganartistsgallery.com

MICHIGANWRITERS
PO Box 2355
Traverse City, MI 49685
michwriters.org

HIGHER ART GALLERY
126 S. Union Street
Traverse City, MI 49684
higherartgallery.com

MARGIN RELEASE BOOKS *IMPROMPTU SERIES*

My Peaceable Kingdom by Lacey Fitch first appeared in the spring issue, Vol. 40, of the *NMC Magazine*, published by Northwestern Michigan College, Traverse City, Michigan. All other visual artwork was part of the "Art in the Peaceable Kingdom" show co-hosted by Michigan Artists Gallery and Higher Art Gallery.

ISBN 978-1-949285-00-0

BOOK DESIGN by Daniel W. Stewart | *daniel@historybydesign.net*

MARGIN RELEASE BOOKS is an imprint of
History By Design
PO Box 1224
Traverse City, Michigan 49685
www.marginreleasebooks.com

PEACEABLE KINGDOM

Daniel Stewart

The Search for a Peaceable Kingdom

A BRIEF INTRODUCTION

What is peace?

I'm sitting on a farmhouse porch, at a wood dining table we once intended to take to the barn, watching the quiet of a country road: a John Deere tractor pulling a fruit-tree sprayer; a heavy truck with—I count them—*26 wheels*; a neighbor's car. Bees are buzzing around me, probably drawn by the flowers of the forsythia and lilacs, which we have allowed to sprawl into unkempt, unconscionable tangles. A chipmunk scurries past my bare feet with a worrisome fearlessness. There has been thunder this morning, and a little rain, and the unstable heaviness that comes with southwesterly winds.

It's a peaceful scene, in other words. Yet there has been violence, too, such as the moment two Novembers ago that still haunts me (and which I recount in "Dominion," my contribution to this collection). It happened only a few feet from where I now sit. As is often the case, I am separated and protected from the violence not by distance but only by time.

This book, as its title promises, is about peace—or, at least, about the *Peaceable Kingdom*, as Edward Hicks called his series of paintings based on three verses from Isaiah, whom Christians regard as the first of the major Old Testament prophets:

> The wolf also shall dwell with the lamb, and the leopard shall lie down with the kid; and the calf and the young lion and the fatling together; and a little child shall lead them. And the cow and the bear shall feed; their young ones shall lie down together: and the lion shall eat straw like the ox. And the sucking child shall play on the hole of the asp, and the weaned child shall put his hand on the cockatrice' den.
>
> — Isaiah 11:6 8 *(King James Version)*

The works collected in this volume, from both visual artists and writers, offer reflections and reactions to the theme of peace that Hicks explored, or to Hicks' paintings, or to Hicks himself; some even react to each other's reactions. This book brings together what we might formally call *ekphrastic* art—art made as a response to visual art—but the organizing principle of this book is informal, even experimental. The mood is most akin to a musical impromptu: flowing from the inspiration of a moment, unpremeditated and without studied care.

That improvisational spirit is also the foundation for this book. Less than three months ago I happened upon the show "Art in the Peaceable Kingdom" co-hosted by Michigan Artists Gallery and Higher Art Gallery, both of Traverse City. Visual artists had created work inspired by Edward Hicks' *Peaceable Kingdom*. The topic seemed as if it might be fruitful and inspiring for writers, too. Could it be possible, during the few weeks that the art show was underway, for writers to join in the artistic response?

I proposed the question as an experiment and also, perhaps, as a challenge. The result—the emphatic YES—you are now holding. This book is evidence of the breadth of writing talent in the Grand Traverse region, as well as testament to the generous spirit of these artists in this corner of northern Michigan.

This volume collects the literary responses to *Peaceable Kingdom*, as well as a number of pieces of visual art from the gallery show. I've included pieces that directly inspired some of the writing, as noted by the writers, as well as other pieces that seem in harmony with the themes raised by the writing. I have also included several of the surviving Hicks paintings themselves, presented in the order that Hicks painted them. The visual art, then, does not serve to illustrate the writing, but stands alongside it as an equal. You might even consider this book as a kind of gallery show of its own.

There are more than 50 voices within these covers, and we offer a host of viewpoints. We have aimed for collaboration, and perhaps we have found some harmony and resonance. I cannot claim that we can offer consensus.

§ § §

PEACE IS NO SIMPLE GOAL, AND WE WISH FOR IT MOST WHEN WE HAVE it least. Edward Hicks painted *Peaceable Kingdom* more than 100 times, but he was not responding to anything like "market demand." He earned nothing from them, giving away each painting to family and friends, and indeed his painting faced active opposition from his fellow Quakers, who considered such "ornamentation" at odds with their devotion to plain customs. Still, he continued to paint. When he died in 1849, aged 69, he was painting yet another version and had been at his easel the night before.

Hicks was obsessed, in other words, and obsession is hardly evidence of peace. The many variations he produced of his *Peaceable Kingdom* were more feral than peaceful; he painted them as jeremiad, not as bucolic reflection. Hicks lived in troubled times, and the troubled faces of "peace" he painted onto his animals—the intelligent goats, the inscrutable wolves, the uneasy lambs, the chafing lions—were images not of satisfaction but of desire. Hicks wanted peace, yes, but he wanted peace of a particular kind.

In his lifetime Hicks was known as a minister rather than a painter, and he seemed to regard his paintings mostly as expressions of his ministry; they were sermons in oils. The Quakers were pacifist but not pacifistic, especially with each other. Hicks was embroiled in the long and often bitter schism between those who wanted to engage with the secular world and those, like Hicks, who wanted to emphasize their connection not to this sinful world but to the Heavenly Kingdom beyond. He painted before, through and after what the Quakers called their Great Separation of 1827, and as the division sharpened so the faces of the animals he painted seemed to grow sharper and more angry—and, finally, weary and perhaps resigned. The Quakers—the Society of Friends—making peace in the background of many of his paintings were there as inspiration and aspiration, not as a reflection. In his painting, Hicks was not intending to reproduce the world as he could see it, because he remained focused upon what his eyes could not see.

Hicks lived in an era filled with violence and injustice, and his conception of peace was not naive. He found a similar voice in the prophet Isaiah. Hicks focused upon the seeming idyll of three resonant verses, but the rest of Isaiah's chapter is full of words like *judge* and *reprove* and *smite* and, finally, *slay*.

Probably *Peaceable Kingdom* resonates with us because we, too, live in troubled times. We are still debating violence and injustice, which means we are arguing about the meaning and the price of peace. In the great struggle of the last generation, Martin Luther King, Jr., was jailed after peaceful protests for *disturbing the peace*—and the irony was on point. The great obstacle to freedom, he wrote from the jail in Birmingham, is the person "who prefers a negative peace which is the absence of tension to a positive peace which is the presence of justice."

The animals in Edward Hicks' *Peaceable Kingdom*—his *Peaceable Kingdoms*—often look unsettled; there is tension within the frame. You will find that same tension throughout these pages.

It seems fitting that we find here more questions than answers. Edward Hicks died about 170 years ago—and Isaiah perhaps 2,500 years before him—and we are still, all of us, asking, *What is peace?*

I OWE THANKS TO EACH PERSON YOU'LL FIND IN THE TABLE OF CONTENTS, whether listed as writer or visual artist, whose accomplishments and talent are exceeded only by their generosity. I also owe special thanks to Sue Ann Round of the Michigan Artists Gallery, for supporting this collection as an idea and in practice; to Shanny Brooke of Higher Art Gallery; to Michigan Writers, Inc.; and to Amanda Holmes, Teresa Scollon and Char Bickel for asking the questions that allowed me to turn a loose idea into an actual book.

Let's do this again, yes?

June 2018

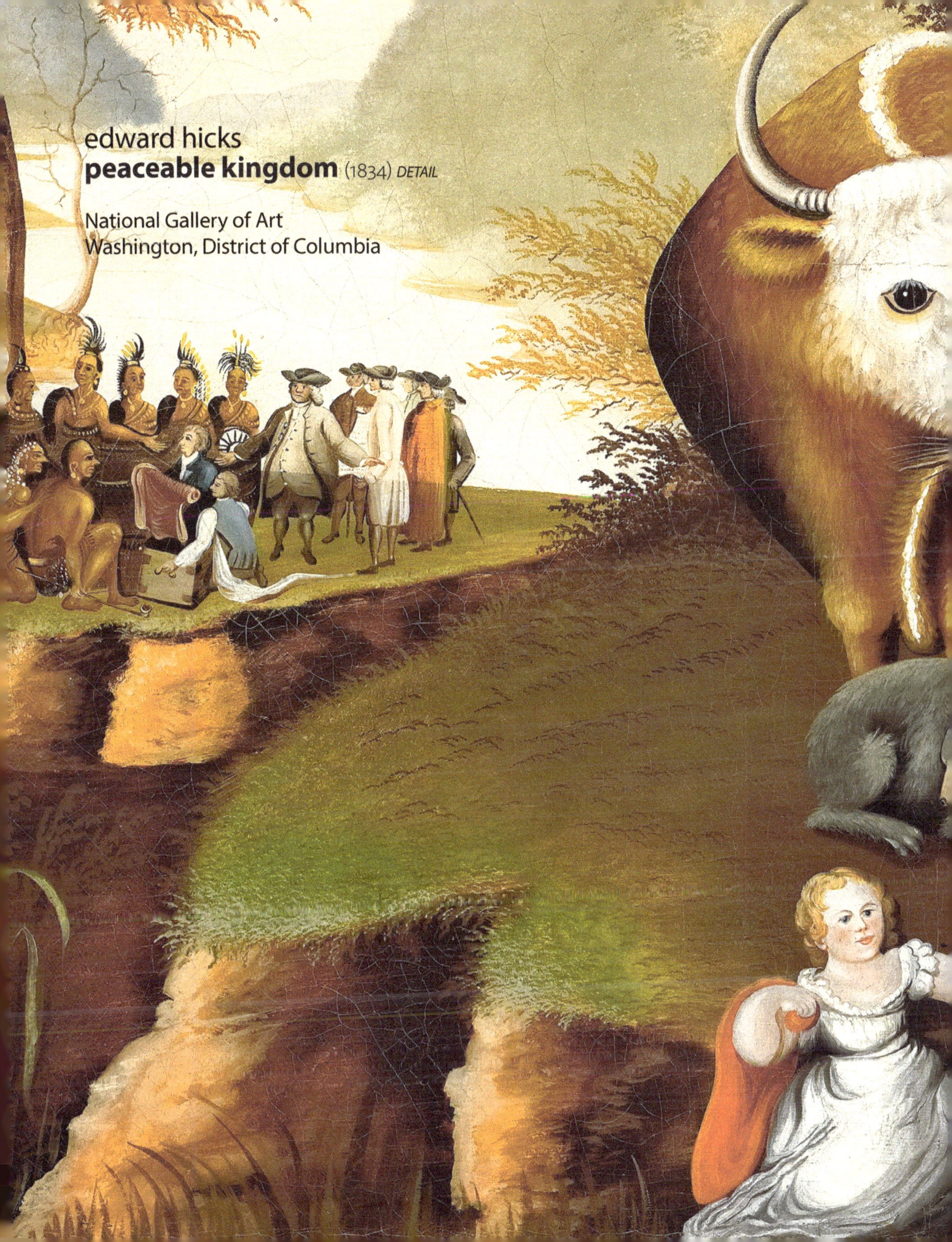

edward hicks
peaceable kingdom (1834) *DETAIL*

National Gallery of Art
Washington, District of Columbia

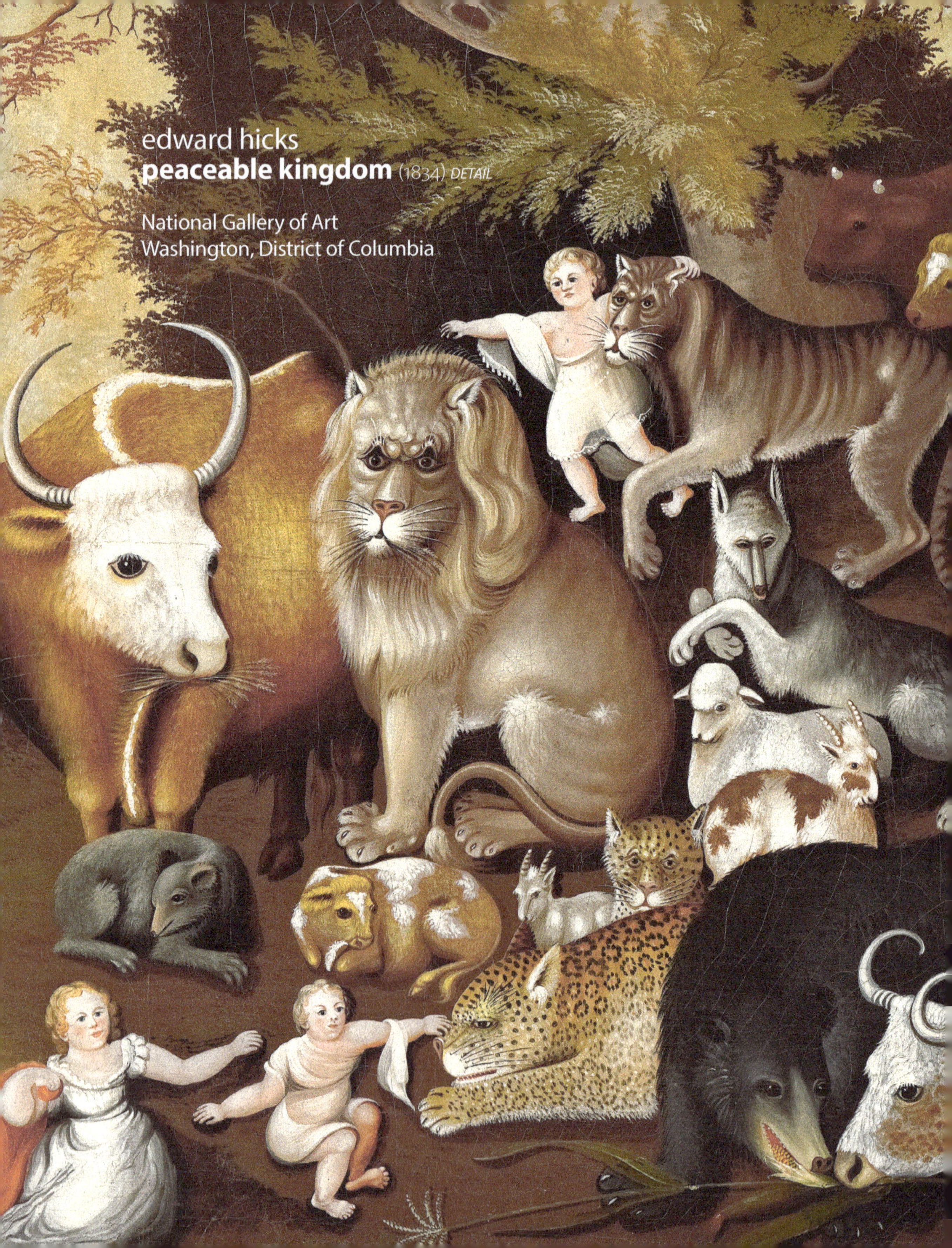

edward hicks
peaceable kingdom (1834) *DETAIL*

National Gallery of Art
Washington, District of Columbia

Robb Astor

LOST AGAIN AMONG THE CREATURES

oh round-horned bull i can't escape the thought
of being alone on the road the village abandoned
the delicate lances of an oryx nearly ran me through
i knew no man was there to speak against my trespass
the sun had turned the buildings grey my dearest
cherub is it not the grasses that hold our world intact
that weave around the antelope and wolf that entwine
the lion the young doe only fleeing for her life
such terror i stepped from my car to stand by the barn
it seemed my eyes had made the distance stir
i thought she was a crowned crane a hundred sheep
had come surrounding me with certainty and welcome
but now i'm lost again among the creatures asking
who is the leopard and who the gazelle oh wide-eyed
lion what encircles this kingdom what binds us
together in this place where all we leave behind
is jagged and white—again and again it's green
that returns

alan maciag

feeding the two hundred

acrylic
23"x 27"

My reaction to Edward Hicks' painting *Peaceable Kingdom* evokes the harmonious relationship between a local gentleman farmer and his Scottish Highland sheep. My painting can have a secular, as well as a biblical meaning. Service to others is one of the most important and rewarding things that we can do with our lives.

This sheepherder can be found at the end of his "normal" workday gathering his flock. He is about to bring peace and harmony to them, by meeting their basic needs of food and shelter, as he calls them by name.

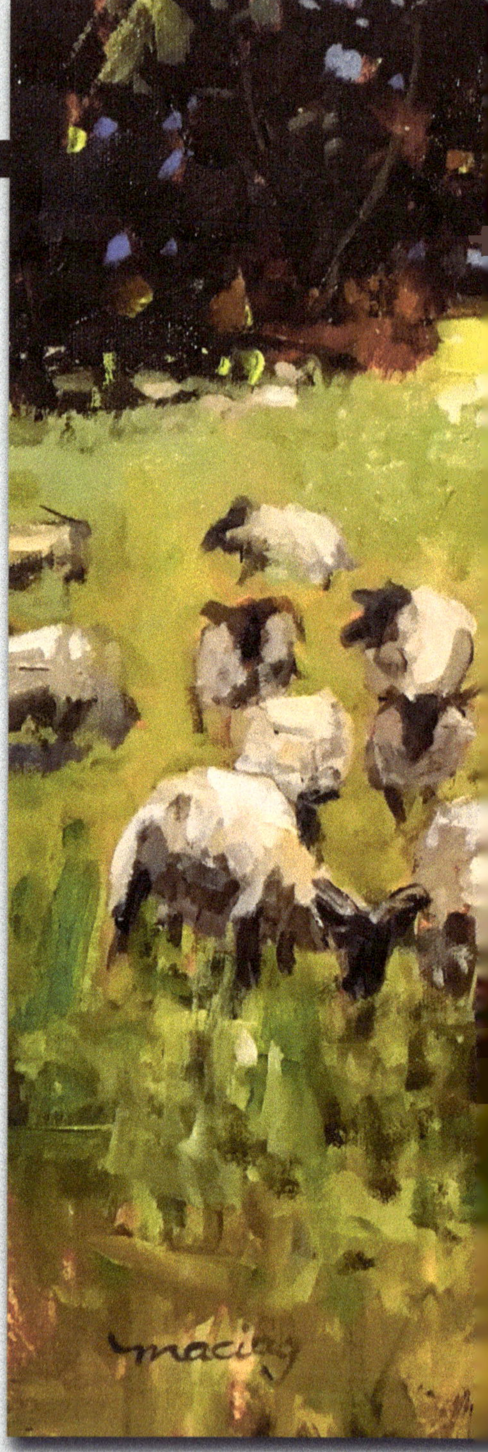

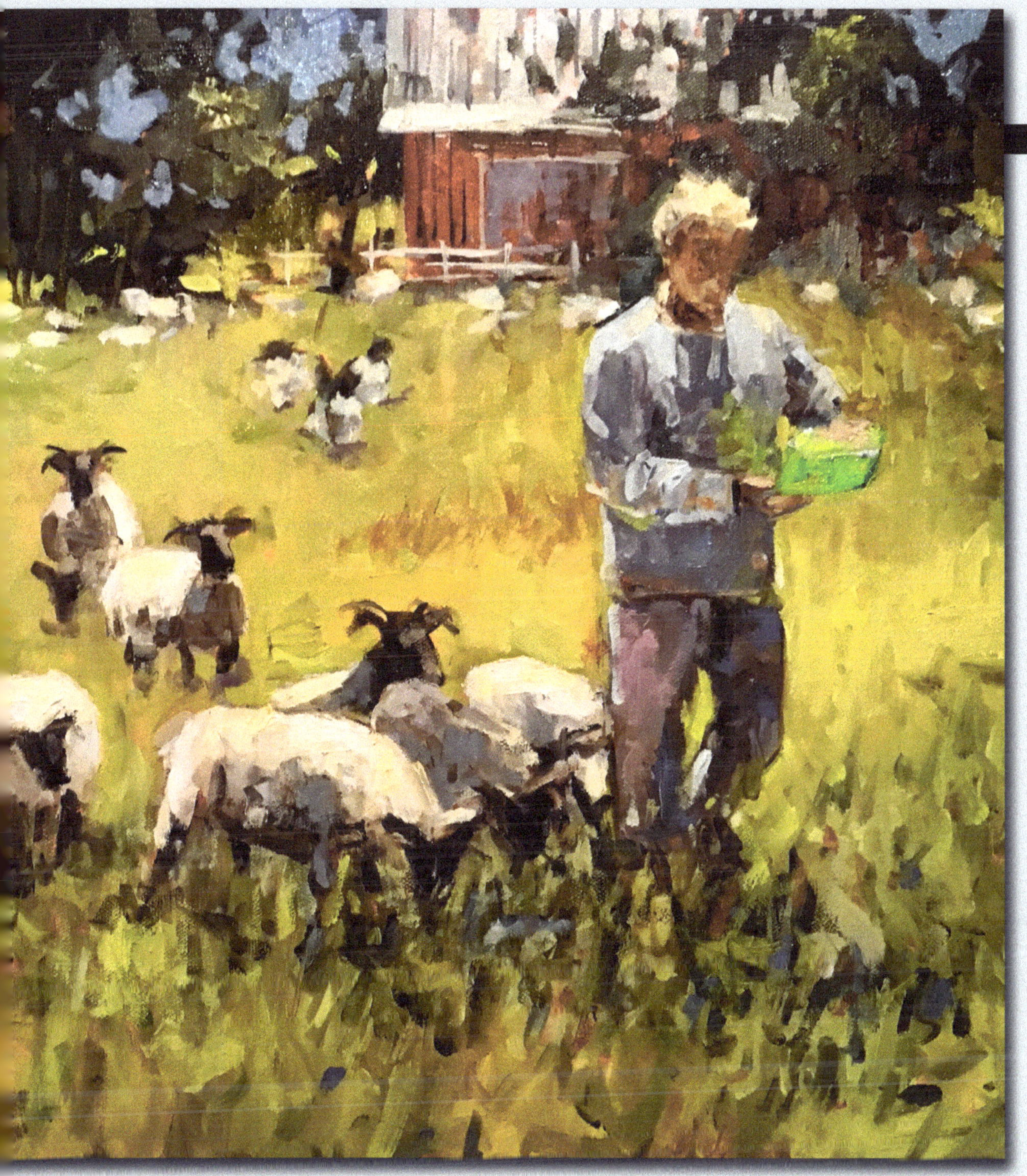

Jennifer Sperry Steinorth

Ode to Creatures Not Appearing In *Peaceable Kingdoms*

I know we're not designed
to be hounds down on all fours
nose to the ground to find
what has fled us. I've tried.
It's hard on the shoulders.

Even in downward facing dog—
        after years of advanced ballet training
        hours daily   rehearsing a romance
        that maintains   women
        above all   should be ethereal—

in down facing dog
        a pose I can hold   a long time
        strong still   and disciplined
        if not also more flexible than
        for my own good—

down dog— yes—
        that most stabilizing inversion
        wherein palms become paws
        to make a quadruped of peace
        and equilibrium   I am prone

to overextension:
slippage:
as every bridge

contract

treaty

does eventually:

collapse.

~

In my book Yoga is a treat.
There aren't many men in my class.

Have you noticed the lack
of adult women in Hicks' numerous Peaceable Kingdoms?

We are easy to miss.
Think of soldiers
in foreign lands
passing nights in a damp trench

nothing but fantasy
and one good hand
(wandering goat, fellow footman)
to entreat.

Even we   misplace ourselves
entirely. As if fallen
into a crevasse. As if a crevasse.

For my next trick I shall become
my own absence.

~

The children in Hicks' paintings
look as though sprung fully frocked
from just such a darkness, one child
always angling to return.

Or else sprung from the toothless grin
of a stymied leopard, of lion—
beasts with whom I too identify—
            in alternate turns tired
            and furious. Ravenous.
            With excellent hair.
                        Ready to gut
                        the horned ungulate
                        mawing in my ear
                                    on what tender herb
                                    he was designed
                                    to stomach.

Or caught in a placating headlock
by a would-be delicious child.

A crevasse is always hungry.
A bloodhound can find anything
except what was never there.

In the studio women double
down, inhale what cant be seen.
We are crow, crane, wild thing,
many dogs, yes—cow.
Frog and crocodile.
Cat and pigeon.
Peacock
scorpion
camel
turtle
fish.
Lion's breath.

We sweat.

We keep the lights dim
and hunt for nothing.
Afterwards we mop
the floors with bleach.

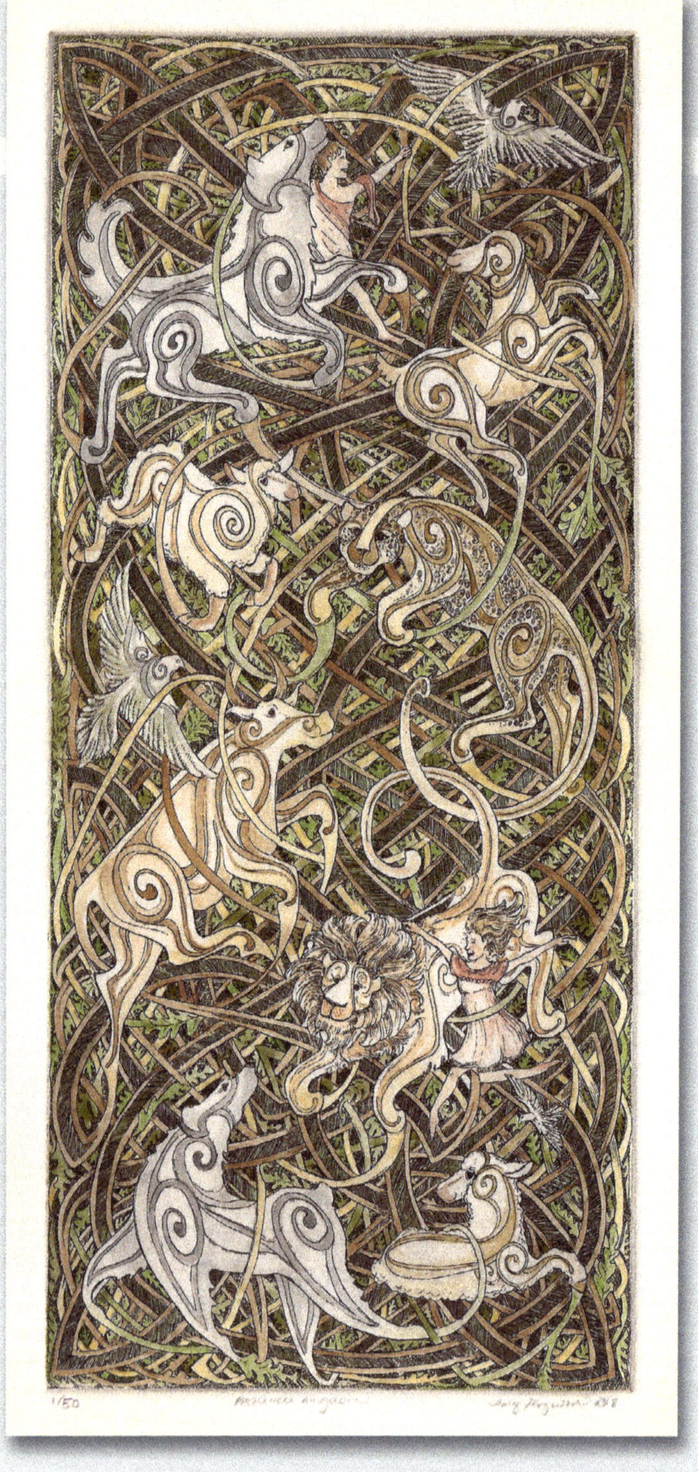

amy ferguson

peaceable kingdom

intaglio copperplate etching
14″x 9″

My three loves, nature, fantasy, and ornamentation, are the subjects I return to for every illustration I create. I love telling stories, and drawing detailed imagery that encourages you to take a second look! Along my way, I found that intaglio etching was the answer I'd been looking for, and lends itself perfectly to my detailed drawings, making it possible to immortalize them in copper, to then create prints. Using this centuries old technique, I am able to create accessible artwork, illustrations that can take anyone to a new place, or an old memory.

For my *Peaceable Kingdom* illustration, I wanted to pay specific attention to the interaction between the animals, and the world that surrounds them in the original painting. I decided to return to one of my favorite ornamentation designs, knot-work, and create an interwoven world of animals and plants, including two children along for the ride. When it came time to add color, I looked to the original painting for inspiration as well.

With leaps of the animals and loops of the plant-knots I like to think I succeeded in making my own little *Peaceable Kingdom*.

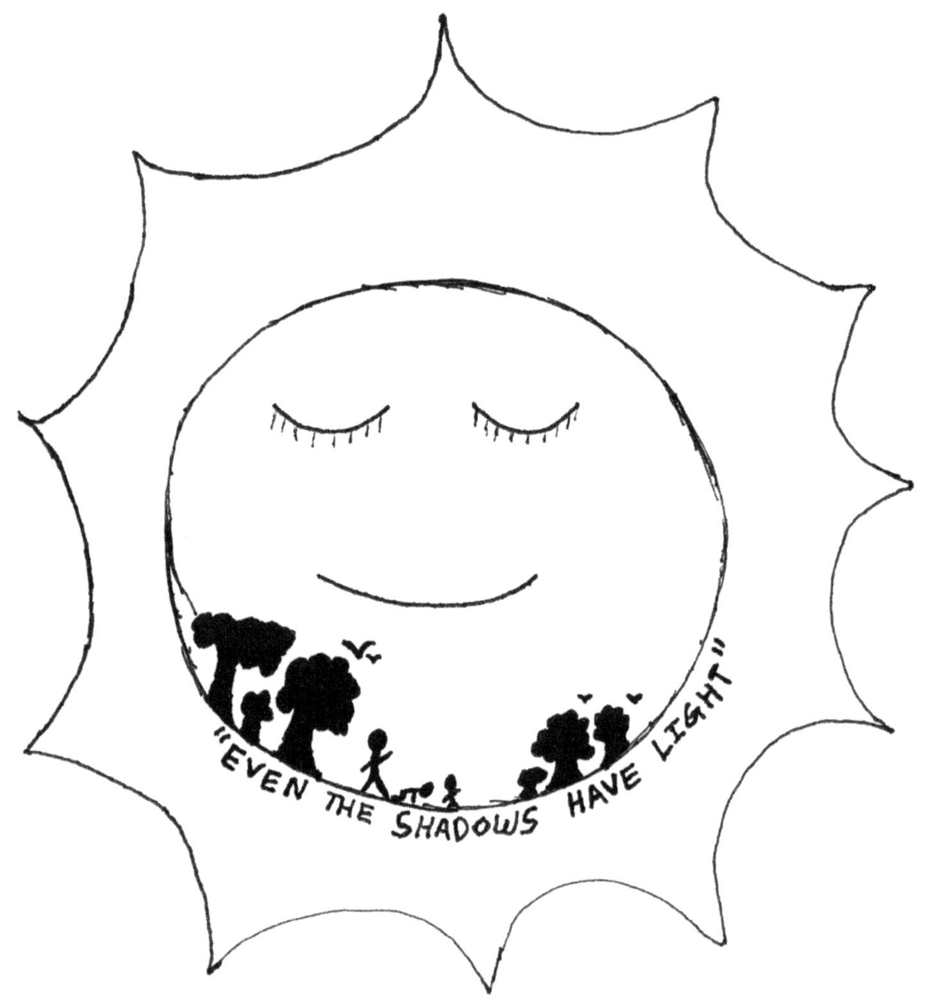

Illustration by Spencer Nye

Spencer Nye

In This Kingdom

In this kingdom, even the shadows have light
The sky is dancing and stars shine bright
No such thing as a foe, no such thing as a frown
No feeling intimidation, only feeling proud
Go pet the lion, for he only wants a kiss
Play with the snake, hear his loving hiss
The water mimics the face of the world
The shark smiles big, showing off his white pearls
Laughter is the language in which we speak
Love is the comforter with which we sleep
My neighbor, my friend, I call you my family
I'd love it if you would stand close here beside me
Nightmares no more, so sleep little child
And when you awake, there's no need to cry.
Open the truth and close out the lies
Open your heart and open your mind
Open your eyes and witness this sight
No need for fear
Because in this kingdom
Even the shadows have light

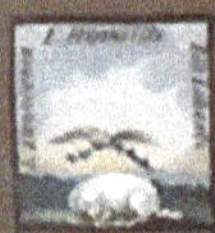
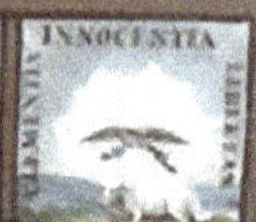

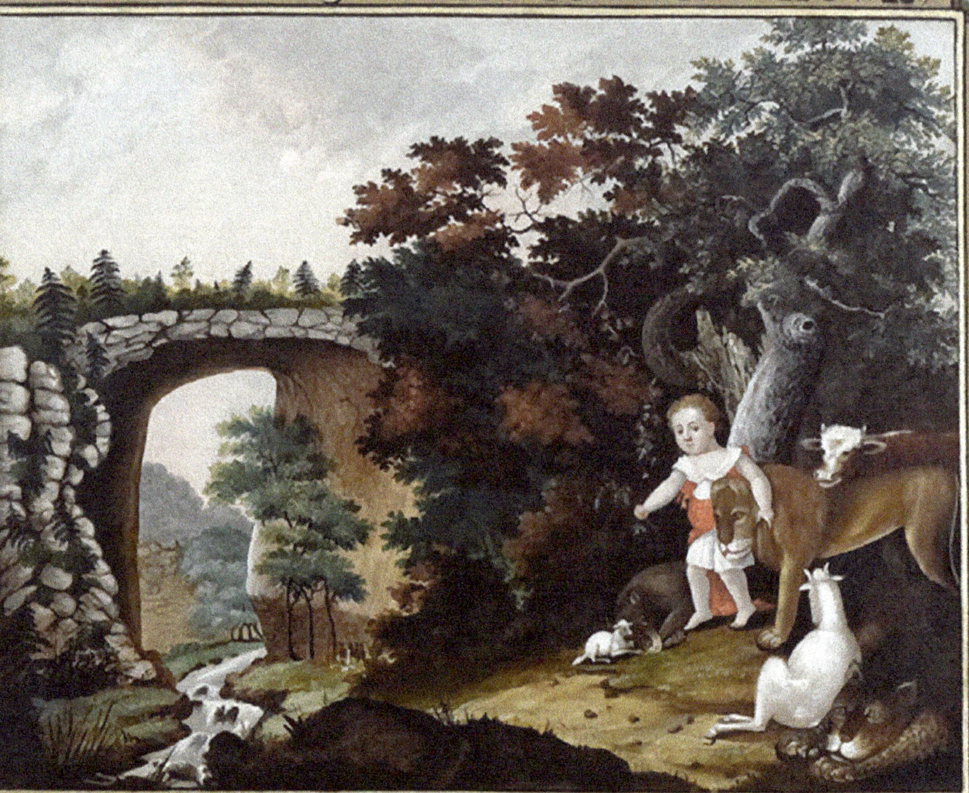

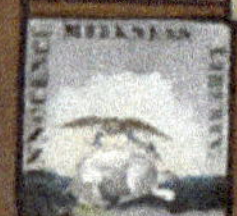

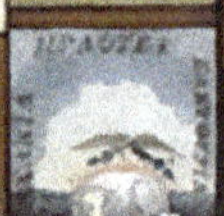

edward hicks
peaceable kingdom (ca. 1822-1825)

Mead Art Museum, Amherst College
Amherst, Massachusetts

Teresa Scollon

A Search for Peaceable Words

Once a student at the college told me he'd gotten frustrated while working on his truck, and rather than make a stupid move in anger, he'd put down his tools, picked up a gun, went out and blasted a chickadee to pieces.

He knew the bird was a chickadee. He knew its name.

We were standing in a hallway after class. His friend was standing next to him. I felt very small in comparison to these tall, robust boys. My heart spoke to me in a short, pained flutter. There was a need to speak. I said I could not help but notice that in order not to harm an inanimate object, he had destroyed a living creature. I said it gently. I was afraid.

We talk this way to each other so rarely that when we do it seems like a new language, one shot through with spaces. He looked at me. He said it was the way he was raised.

Questions hung in the air. Somehow we made our way to a little table. He wanted to know why I thought the way I did. I wanted to know why he thought the way he did, but I didn't dare push too hard. I was afraid we would lose each other. I wanted us to stay open.

He was a nice boy.

My words sounded so inadequate, puny. I said I felt that there were so many creatures, and there must be a reason why; there was a mystery greater than we could know, and I wanted to respect it. He listened. He said, it's probably wrong, but it's the way he was raised. Repetition. Pause.

His friend watched us, listened, said nothing. We were courteous, all three. We went our separate ways. I have never forgotten it.

At a dinner party last year a man, an artist, a retiree, a nice man, told me he spread poison for spiders on the outside of his house. He did not say poison. He said product, some kind of product, to keep away spiders. Because they make it hard to clean the windows.

Another woman says her neighbors want to kill a fox that lives on the edges of her subdivision. Because it lives. Another man has a problem with moles tearing up his lawn.

We are so casual about this killing. I think, I am over fifty years old; I have been living through an age of mass extinction. We keep building houses in forests, we keep pouring cement, we keep buying and driving, we keep shoving animals out of the way. Repetition. But we love animals, so we write poems of grief, we paint pictures. It is senseless. I can't understand why anyone would kill just to get something out of the way. And because I don't understand I must be careful when I speak. I am filled with fury, and the bridge between people is so narrow. Then I think, I am a coward compared to the little fox, out hunting to feed her kits, defenseless against the casual violence of men. I don't know how to speak about it beyond naming the names of the lost.

There is no language that changes us.

In despair, I look up the definition of "word". It says the stability of a word's meaning permits mutual comprehension. It says a word is the smallest unit of meaning. In pieces, a chickadee is no longer a chickadee. But we both know what it used to be. Words name what we know, are the means by which human knowledge is fixed in memory and transmitted in speech.

Human knowledge: Chickadee.

Memory: Fox.

To be spoken aloud: Spider.

I am so afraid we will lose everything. My heart races. My tongue is stilled.

■

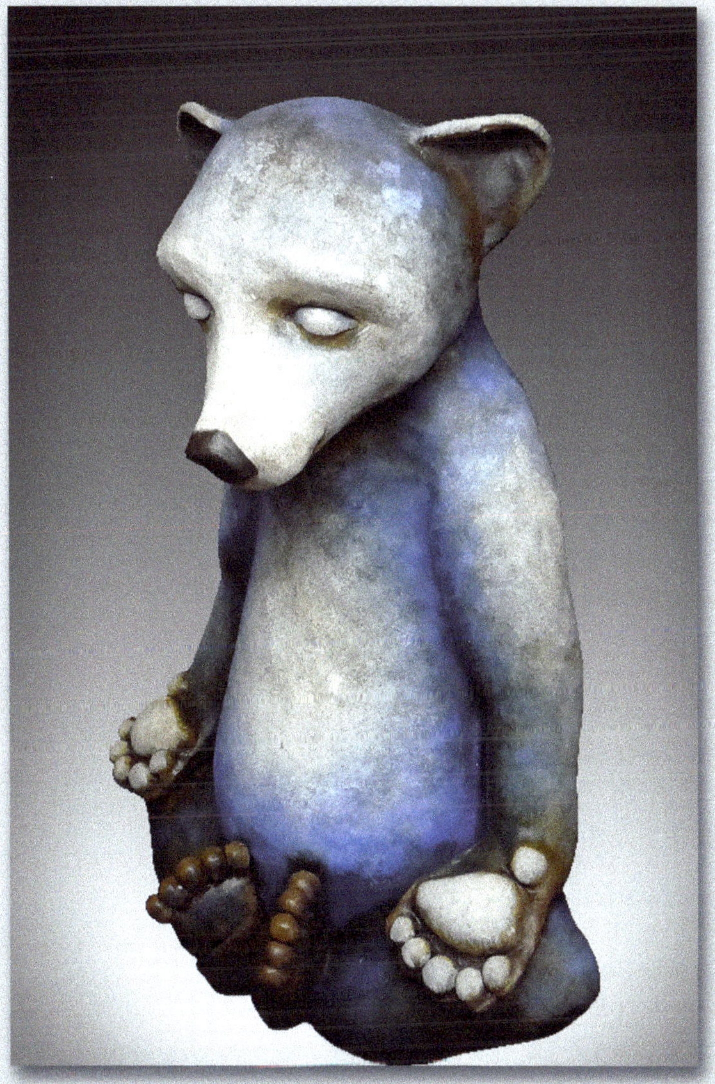

leanne schnepp

blue bear: vishudda

stoneware clay, stained & glazed
20" x 11" x 8"

The Vishuddha, truth or blue chakra, is located in the throat area. This fifth chakra is thus related to communication, creativity and expression. Opening this fifth chakra allows you to speak the truth. When we know and can speak our truth with love and compassion, we can create a more peaceful self and thus a more peaceful world. Namaste.

Fleda Brown

Peaceable Kingdom

While I was helping you adjust your infernal
brace, bring you your water, your pills, and prop
your feet, I was thinking that the idea of utopia
is adolescent: paradise never works out.
The lion lies down with the lamb and the lion's lids
twitch with anticipation. Lions are lions. Lambs
are lambs. Nothing holds still. Imagine peace.
Don't you think of a *trompe l oeil?* Animals all
balanced, curve matching curve, horns, paws.
As if they were drugged. I am tired of waiting
for paradise. I thought it was possible once.
I was a child of the 50s. You can see how I might.
Between wars. Then seemingly from beneath,
the grumble and roar, claws pulling the whole
swamp-creature up through a widening crack.
When you get rid of one thing, it isn't gone.
What's left yearns, of course, for its mate.
What to do then? As if there were something.
I trace your spine. It is like one of Paul Klee's
line drawings, bent and bent until you see it's
meant to be a back, however damaged.
However damaged, it's an electric highway,
energetic as a wire spring, like the line drawings.
Klee's biographer Lazzaro says Klee found his
true climate in the zone between "the active
forces of mutation and destruction."

Okay, the peaceable kingdom, poised there,
is not nothing. The lion pretends to love
the lamb, and does, complexly. It is all so
complex, the loving, let's call it that.
When framed, it can be aesthetically grand.

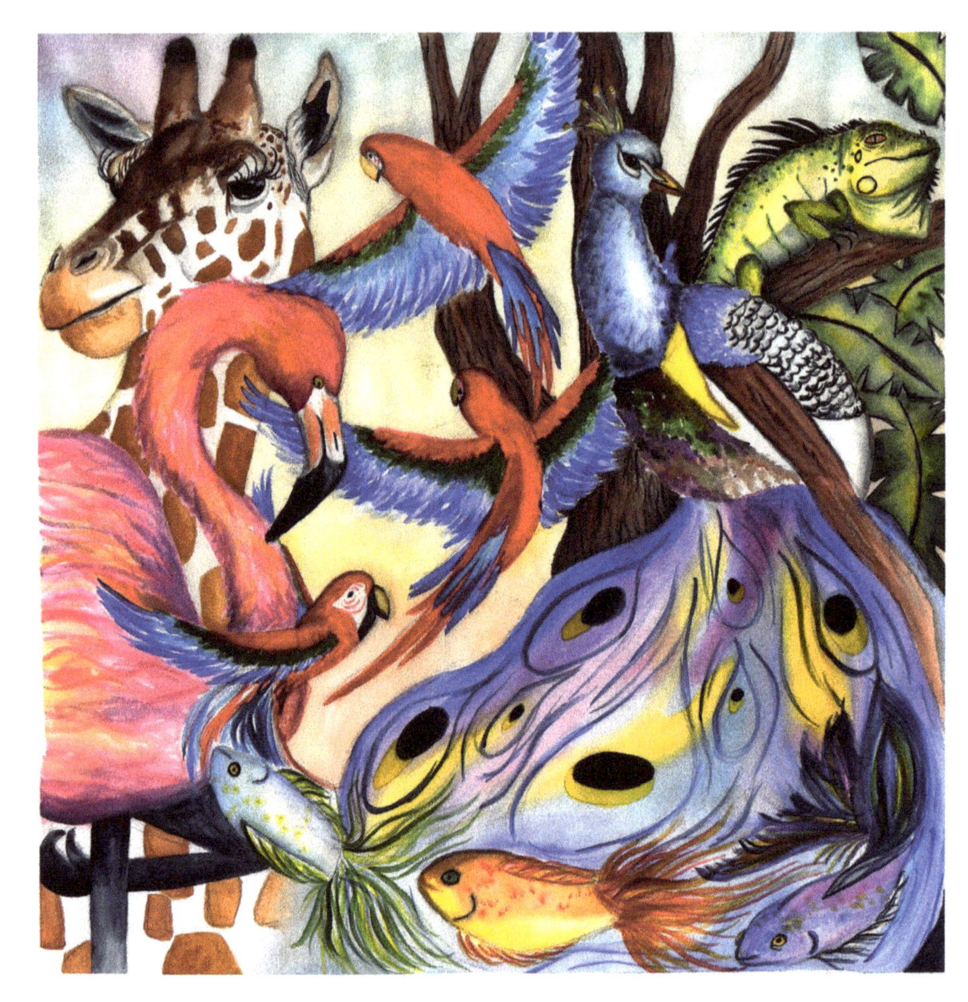

lacey fitch

my peaceable kingdom

watercolor

I am a student at Northwestern Michigan College. *My Peaceable Kingdom* is a watercolor and was inspired by all of God's beautiful creatures and the amazing qualities they possess. I have always loved the unique beauty animals have, and I named my piece after it reminded me of Edward Hicks' *Peaceable Kingdom*.

Elaine Mcintosh

Sustainability

I heard, but did not see the bear
as he lumbered up the four steps to my porch
something propelled him to grab the birdfeeder,
swing from the wrought iron pole, twisting
it out of all its sculpted beauty—possum, owl,
coyote or raccoon also wondering
in the dark moonless night
the young brown bear, seeking his territory
ran next to the wild blueberry patch
now diminished by my
newly built two car garage.
I do not begrudge the twisted pole—
a beloved gift—
sharing the bewilderment of stumbling
out of a favorite shady woods
into the sun of my favorite beach
finding the white sand occupied by
adults, children, beach chairs and kites,
dogs, and umbrellas. Uprooted, I,
wander back into the woods,
searching for what I remembered
as my own.

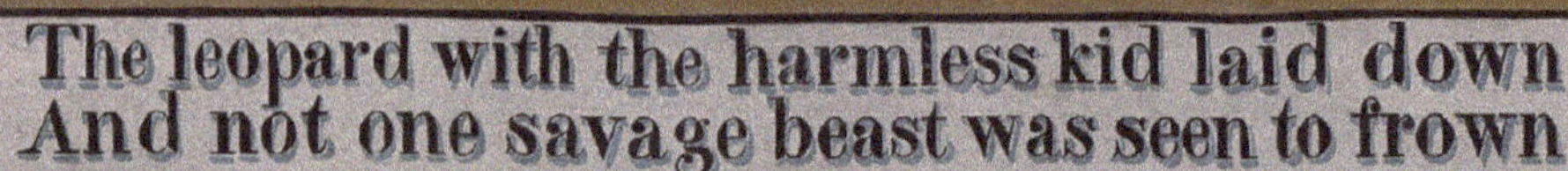

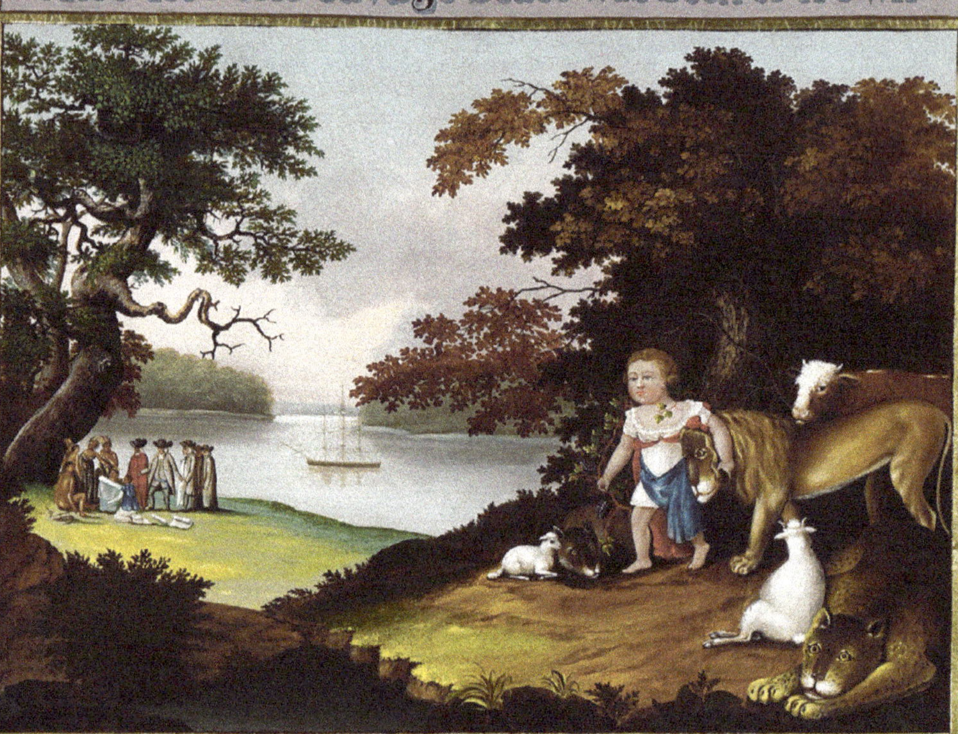

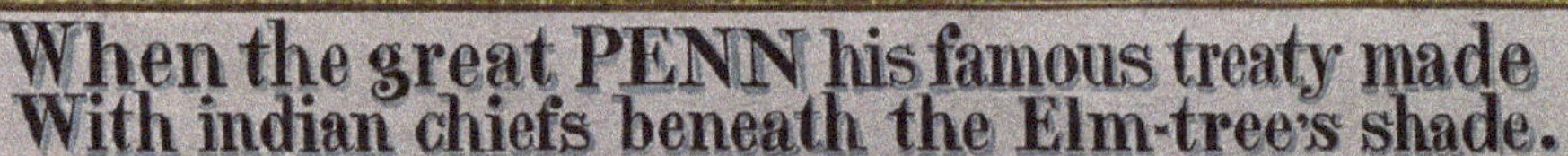

edward hicks
peaceable kingdom (ca. 1826)

Philadelphia Museum of Art
Philadelphia, Pennsylvania

Bob McQuilkin

The Peaceable Kingdom

Look what I found. Looks like an old photograph of a wedding party. You can tell the photographer staged the whole thing. Looks like a family that doesn't get along very well. Probably only get together for weddings and funerals. Not a very friendly bunch. Some aren't even looking at the camera. Look at the eyes. Staring vacantly. And their expressions. The photographer probably forgot to say "cheese." Children were invited. They look nothing like their parents. That is the flower girl hanging on to her mother, who must be the maid of honor. The bride and groom look indifferent. They probably already had their first quarrel. The bridesmaids are anxious to get it over with. They are hungry. The reception is down by the lakeshore. See, the guests are gathering. The groom's family is decked out in fancy clothes. Look like they are more ready for a meeting than a party. The bride must have had native Americans in the family. Bet that raised some eyebrows. Wonder if the groom's family knew. Let's see how long those two families get along.

Found the photo while cleaning out the basement. My parents were friends of the groom. See them there looking like lost sheep? That is certainly a mangy crew. You know what they say. "Birds of a feather flock together." I know there aren't any birds in the photograph. You know what I mean. Those characters don't belong together. I am sure that marriage did not last long.

leanne schnepp

malala yousafzai: nobel peace prize winner 2014

stoneware clay bust, stained & glazed
13″ x 10″ x 21″

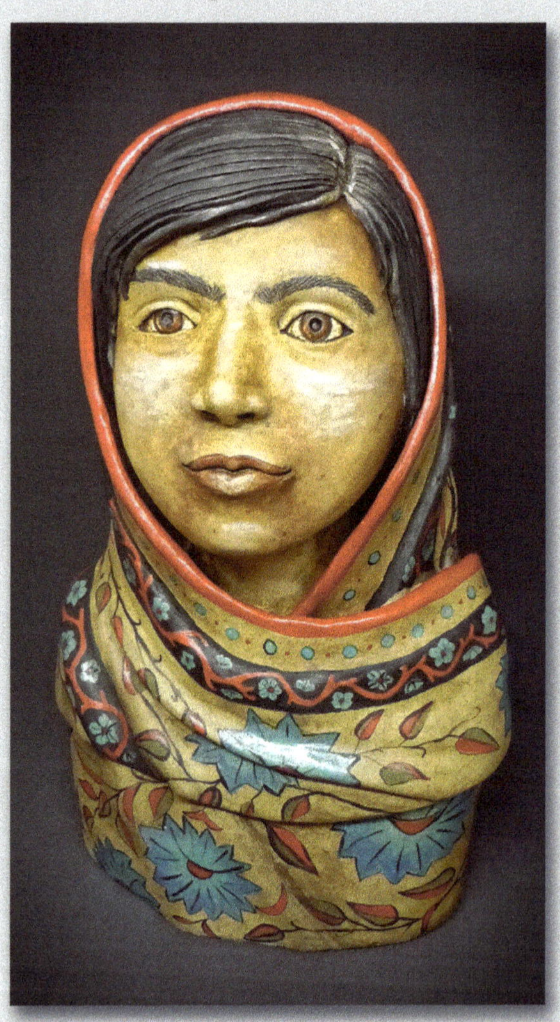

Malala Yousafzai is a Pakistani education advocate who, at the age of 17, became the youngest person to win the Nobel Peace Prize. She was awarded the prize along with Indian activist Kailash Satyarthi. Malala was named by her father after a legendary 19th Century Pashtun warrior heroine, Malalai of Maiwund. Her father being an educator, she understood the value of education, especially for women, while living in Pakistan after the Taliban occupation. When Malala was 11 years old, the Taliban banned girls from attending school. This fueled her drive to promote girls' education around the world. "I truly believe the only way we can create global peace," she said, "is through not only educating our minds, but our hearts and souls." Creating a bust of Malala Yousafzai was a great challenge and honor. I wanted to communicate the importance of this living hero but at the same time depict her as a young girl who has sacrificed much. She shows her physical injuries in her eyes, one eye being larger than the other. She continues to work to bring peace and education to girls around the world.

John Pahl

Your Point of View

--Our Father, whose art's in heaven?

I entered the gallery a bit on edge. I needed to make my visit brief, with a daughter to pick up at school within an hour at most. But the gallery was a small one, and I would focus mostly on the centerpiece to the exhibit—a copy of Hicks' *Peaceable Kingdom* and a variety of regional artists' responses to that iconic painting.

I'd seen the painting on a small scale in any number of art history textbooks, a few reproductions of it in various church lobbies, and even once on a giant billboard shortly after leaving Michigan and entering Indiana, that billboard having been followed by a series of others asking, in slightly different ways, if I and all the other drivers heading south on I-69 had been saved—or not.

So I went directly to the Hicks reproduction and saw, again, the collection of domesticated and wild animals reposing on the grass in a clearing backing up to a deep woods, then across the way, on what seemed like an island of grass almost floating in air, an assembly of men, whites and Indians, they seemed, like the animals, clustered together and not fighting, not killing each other.

After just a moment of contemplating this larger version of the familiar image, I felt a nudge on my elbow. I turned to see a very attractive woman, smiling and holding out a plastic cup of red wine. I'd seen but had walked past a refreshment table with the wine and a few plates of cheese and crackers, thinking I'd show an interest in the art before grabbing the offerings.

"You missed the wine," this woman said, smiling and pressing the cup into my hand. She had jet-black, very shiny hair, which just then she tossed, with a clever shift of her head, from one bare shoulder to another. Beneath her shoulders, her dress shimmered a deep purple—I guess it was purple—but it seemed to have a glitter to it on the surface and a smoldering red hue just beneath that purple glitter, almost like coals waiting there to return to full flame.

"Thanks," I managed to say, returning her smile. Her eyes bore deeply into mine in that moment of my awkwardness about what to say next. Those eyes had a glitter, too, but a dark glitter.

I managed to get out an "Umm—" when she asked, "What do you make of this exhibit, the Hicks and these responses to it? Do you mind my asking?"

"No, not at all," I answered. I sipped my red wine to gain a moment. "It's surprisingly good, this wine," I said, lifting my glass. "I haven't really looked at the responses to the Hicks painting yet. But I can see already that this full-sized copy of his painting offers more than the reproductions I've seen in books or on those post cards, you know the kind, the ones with famous art on them sold in museum gift shops. I once bought a card, in fact, with this very—"

"Yes. Well, you need to take the right point of view to appreciate his painting," she interrupted.

"It all depends on your point of view." She turned her face from the direction of the painting and gave me another direct look, her eyes even more intense now.

"Well, that makes sense," I replied. "After all, a devout Christian will see this painting quite differently than, say, an atheist, or even an agnostic would. Agreed?" I found myself shifting closer to her, as though I was getting a better position for viewing the painting.

"Actually," she paused and lifted her face up toward mine, "I didn't mean 'point of view' that way. I meant it literally, not as a philosophical or religious stance, but a physical one." Now she had turned her whole body in my direction, as if we were about to dance or something. "Literally the vantage point of viewing something, as in how close, from what angle, that sort of thing."

"Ok. I get it," I said, perhaps moving myself just a tad in her direction. I could feel, I thought, her warmth across the inches between us.

She nudged my elbow again, her hand staying there for what seemed like several seconds. "Come over here, closer." She led me much closer to the painting, directly in front of it, and I felt guilty knowing that we were blocking others' view of it.

"See how from this range, at this angle, certain details appear that you might miss from a different angle and further back?" She gestured toward the painting and continued. "Look, for instance, at the wolf, if that's what it is, at his muzzle. Notice the red tinge in the hair, especially below his mouth?" I leaned in a bit for a still closer look, and I did see that color there. I was about to say so, when she went on.

"And the big lion. Notice a red smear on his muzzle as well? You can't see that until you get up close, like this, especially at this angle—because of the lighting."

I saw that, too, a smear of red on the lion's hair on either side of his mouth. I was sure that I was even seeing a glistening drop of red at the end on one of his whiskers, though it might have been a highlight of the artist's varnish catching the overhead gallery lights.

"And look closely at the lion's eyes. Have you noticed them before?" She patted my right arm to emphasize her words. "Don't they look absolutely crazy? Like the lion is dizzy, or in a trance, or maybe drugged on something. Don't you think?" Now her tap turned into a soft squeeze on my forearm. That felt good, I had to admit. "Yes, you're right," I said. "I do see what you're showing me. You have to get close to notice it, and maybe only from an angle like this."

I straightened up from my slight tilt toward the painting. "I suppose how he handled the brush strokes and—what do you call it?—his texture, or impasto technique?—might explain that subtle effect. Is that it?"

"Well, whatever his method, it's there if you really take a good look." And she looked back at me, giving me, I thought, a slight wink. "Makes you wonder what Hicks might have painted as a scene just half an hour before this one, maybe back in those dark woods, doesn't it?"

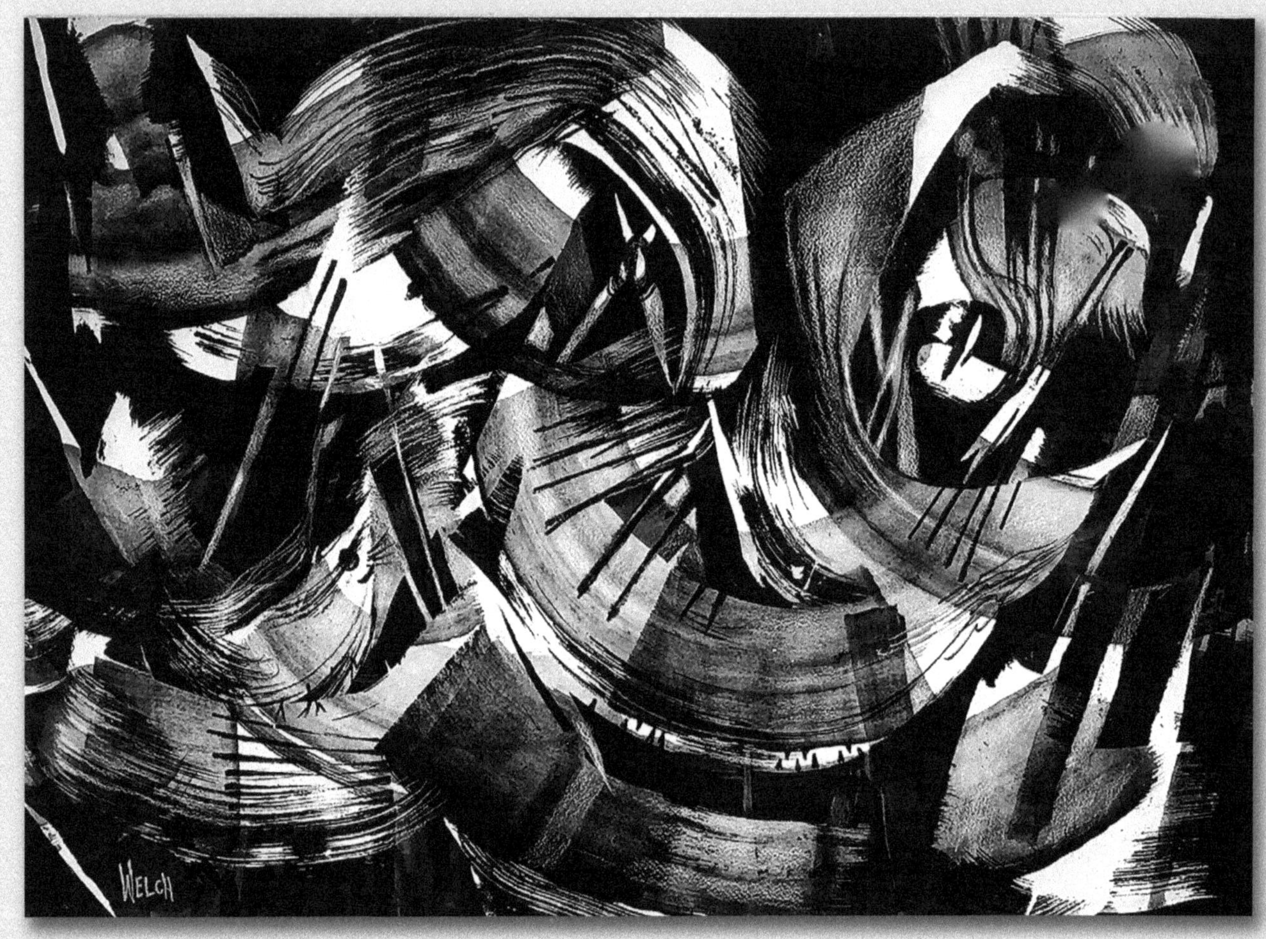

paul welch
the cat & the chickadee

watercolor
21″ x 28″

The day will come when "cats" and "birds" will share the earth when we're gone.

"You mean—"

"Oh, I don't mean anything, really." She glanced around the room, as if I weren't there, within reach. "It's just that I've always thought this painting was absolutely too contrived, too idealized to have achieved the fame it has claimed over the years." She shook her head, her shiny loops of hair swinging across those bare shoulders. "I mean—not to be too cynical or anything—it's as if everyone took the rural paintings of Grandma Moses seriously, as if American farm life has ever been like that—green grass everywhere, ducks strutting around like they were happy or something and not the main course for Sunday dinner waiting to surprise them. No sign of an angry, abusive, drunk farmer and his lonely, fearful wife miles from anyone out there in good ol' American farmland."

She took another long sip of her wine, a drop glistening in the corner of her mouth, where her upper lip met her lower one in an exquisite point, like none other I'd seen before.

"I hope I've not interfered with your appreciation of this wonderful painting," she said, rather dramatically, raising her hands as if in supplication, her wine cup now empty. "but you looked like someone interesting to talk to, to compare notes with." With that she smiled and walked swiftly to the table, deposited her empty plastic up, turned once to give me another look, and was out the door. But it wasn't really the exit of the gallery, the door I'd come in through. It was just a door in the wall between two pieces of Hicks-inspired free-form sculpture. She was gone, just like that.

So I took another long look at *The Peaceable Kingdom*, shrugged for some reason, then gave the other pieces on display a token look, glanced at my watch, returned my cup to the table and left though the front door, stepping into the glare and noise of the busy avenue on which this gallery stood, my car a good two blocks away.

Halfway down the second block I heard a voice to my left and looked. There in a doorway—I think a doorway to a bakery—stood a woman who seemed to be the same woman, but with much shorter hair, and hair that was deep red, real red, not died, I felt immediately. She wore a different dress, too, so, given the brief moments since seeing her depart through some odd door that didn't exit to the sidewalk and this avenue, I was puzzled. But I was also pleased.

She gave me a look like the first one in the gallery, a straight, hard look, as if electricity were behind those eyes, connecting to mine.

"It looks like you're going my way," she said, nodding toward the sidewalk stretching off to the sky at the top of the small hill this avenue was climbing. She smiled irresistibly.

"Yes," I replied. "I'm headed that way, Your way, too, I take it."

■

Anne-Marie Oomen

Poetic Triptych

Here, three poems responding to three artists in the "Art in the Peaceable Kingdom" exhibit at the Michigan Artists Gallery. These three artists' pieces were set in proximity in the gallery, so when I studied them, certain themes began to overlap in my notes. In these, I have probably taken a stance opposite the artists' intent. I hope I don't offend the artists who inspired me, but it seemed to me their artists' statements belied some expressions in their work. Or perhaps some dis-ease under their beautiful surface renderings was speaking, and that aligned with my feeling of skepticism about the *Peaceable Kingdom*. Or perhaps, in light of the news, I was feeling satiric, or simply despairing at the way we look at the peaceable kingdom with such hope and have botched it so badly.

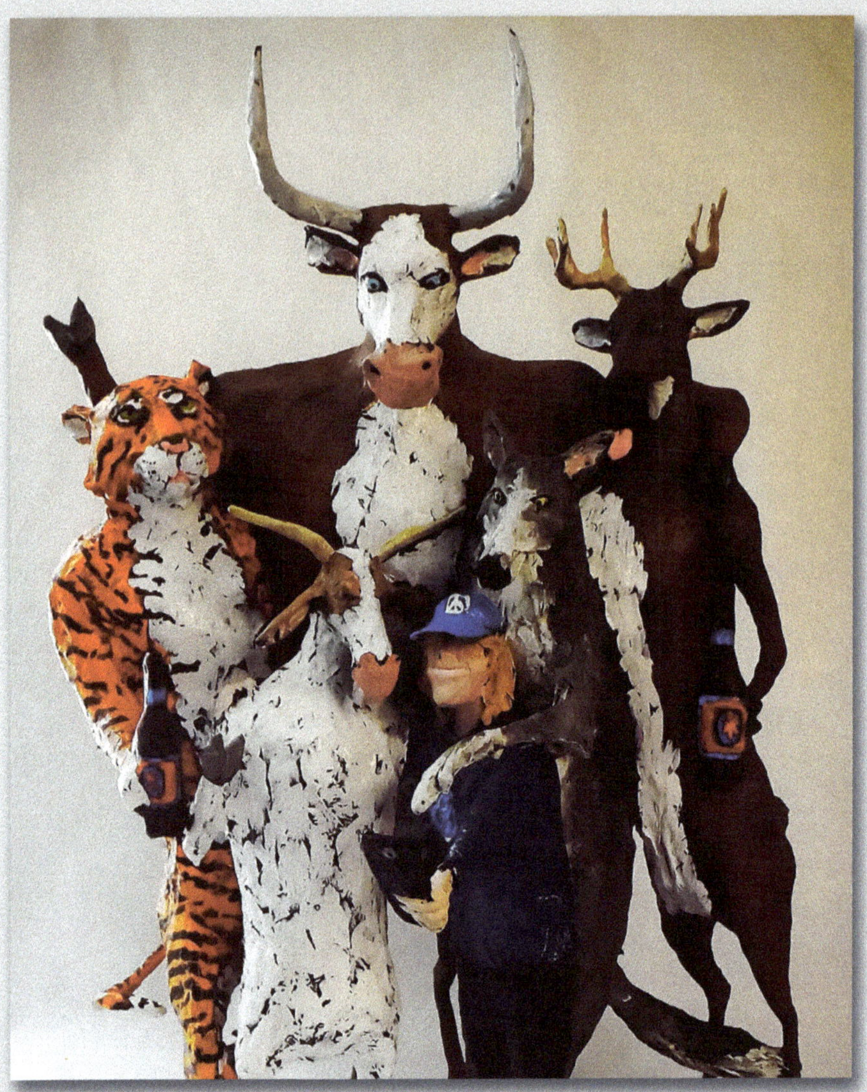

steve wirtz
the sociable kingdom

mixed media
23″ x 17″ x 17″

Maybe if Edward Hicks painted another 62 versions of his vision he would have come up with something similar to this. Okay, maybe not. But aside from getting a little anthropomorphic here, my version suggests what peace between species could really look like in today's modern society.

Anne-Marie Oomen

1. Look Closely at Their Eyes

inspired by *The Sociable Kingdom* by Steve Wirtz

Doesn't that look like fun?
A selfie right there with all those antlered
and beclawed creatures,
guffawing with a good 'ole boy,
hanging out in the local dive,
celebrating the naïve
wonder of the one-time hunter
who kills and blunders, but gosh
have another,

all is forgiven.

Just one of the guys.

Just one of the guys,

as the creatures surround him
back slapping and dirty-joking
and raising a glass,
and toasting
his aim, and toasting his
duplicitous grin, and toasting
him before they cuff him
on the chin, and finally—
just look at their eyes—
do him in.

diane hawkey

peaceable kingdom, a global history of man

ceramic
9″ x 9.5″ x 8″

I tried to find a balance between the 19th century optimism of Edward Hicks and the skepticism of the 21st century. I was deeply affected by the shooting at Stoneman Douglas High School. It made me doubt that there would ever be a peaceable kingdom on this earth, but the activism that was awakened in our young people has reassured me that the world can change and there is hope for a peaceable kingdom.

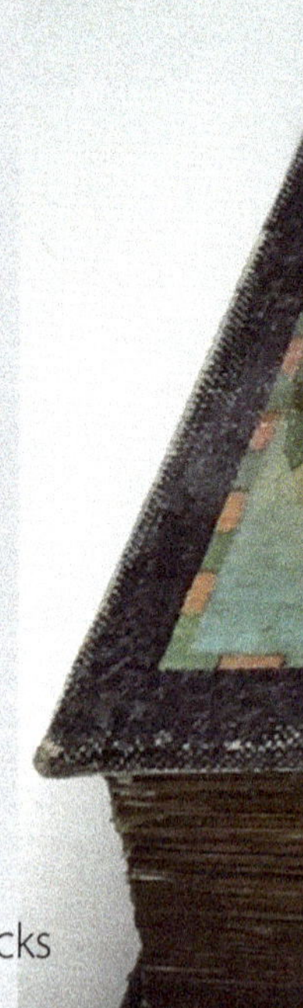

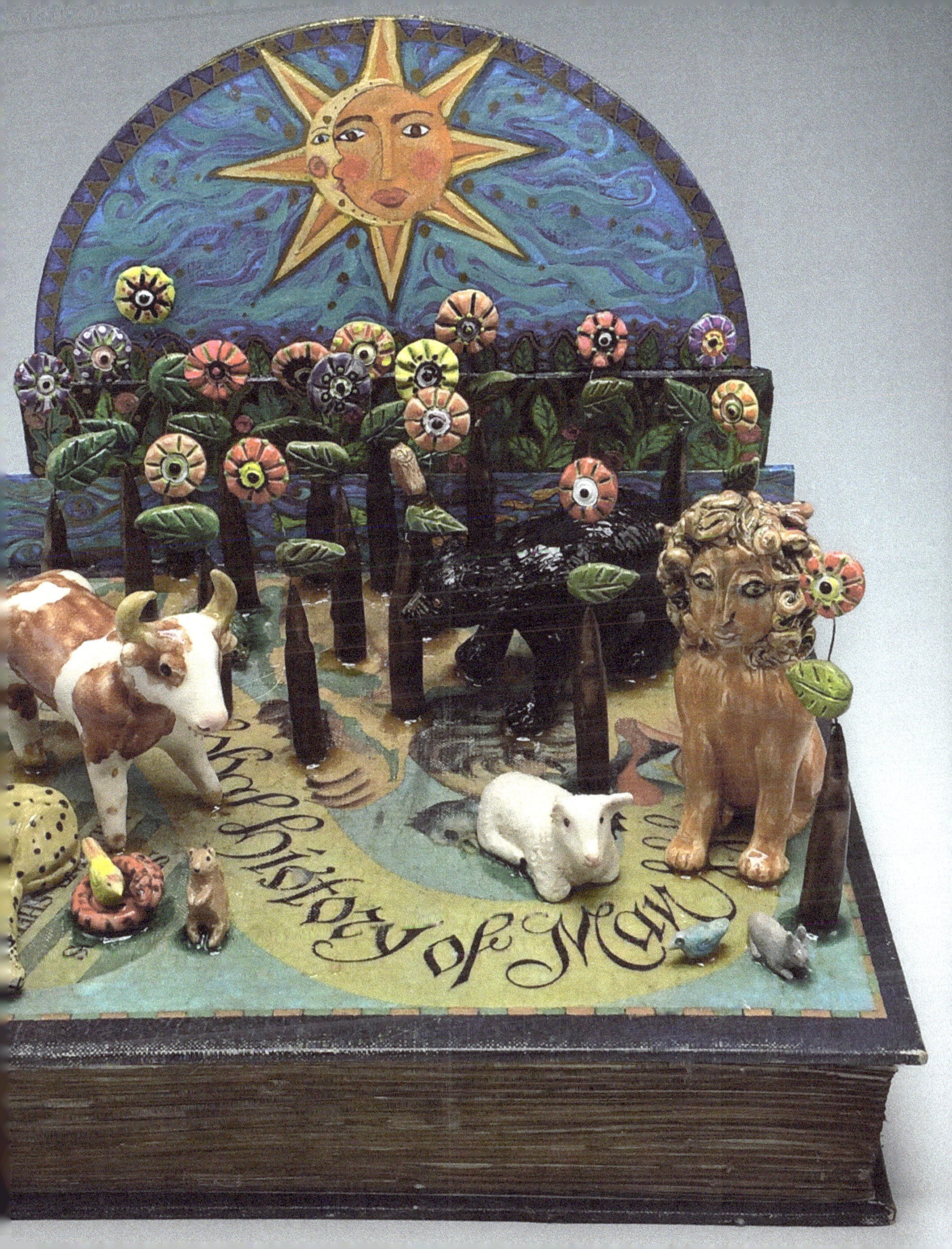
History of Man

Anne-Marie Oomen

2. History of Man

inspired by *Peaceable Kingdom: A Global History of Man* by Diane Hawkey

Under iconic moon and sun,
your mind recognized Kingdom
as sham, thus your hands
made flower stems
of empty casings, seventeen

ruined shells for seventeen
children shot—
all topped with rainbow blooms, set
on paradise's soil, the "ground"
upon which these flowers grew—

History of Man, a book
titled in elegant script
becomes the burial site.
If the title were not shame
enough, you have gathered

the animals, set them
still and mocking
on the leather and paper mass.
They are not feeding,
they stare at us.

Anne-Marie Oomen

3. Utopia 484

inspired by *A Field Guide to the Button Kingdom* by Brian Schorn,
found object assemblage of 484 buttons

Buttons set in lovely rows,
not touching
but aligned, orderly,
respectful even,
multihued, and yes
of course of multiple sizes,
but within a certain range;
yes of course, all round
as an oxen's docile eyes—
no lions, no squares
invited here—
and not one is screaming
at the others,
and each is stitched
to its own place,
and all together
the whole pattern
is courteous, the rims
prettily embossed,
and it doesn't matter
which one has two
or four holes, all depends
on purpose, though none seems
purposeful at this moment.
At last a Peaceable Kingdom

I can get behind.

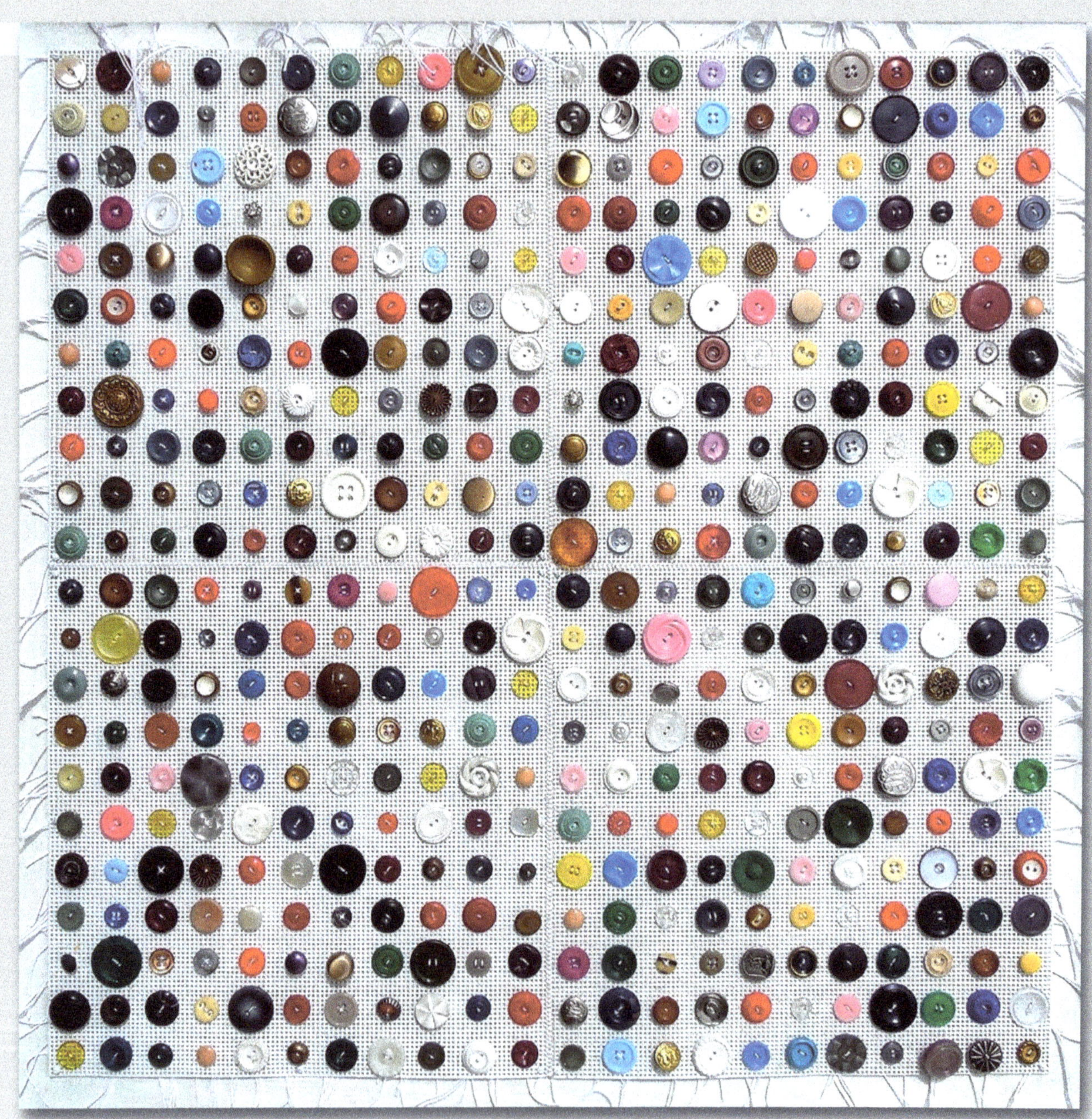

brian schorn

a field guide to the button kingdom

found object assemblage
24" x 24"

A Field Guide to the Button Kingdom is a loose interpretation of the Quaker beliefs and ideals of American folk painter Edward Hicks as seen in his painting *Peaceable Kingdom*. Hicks began his career as a distinguished religious minister but ultimately chose to express his beliefs through his paintings. The Inner Light doctrine as preached by the Quakers, is depicted in Hicks' paintings as a breaking down of physical barriers so that everyone can live and work together in peace and harmony. In other words, Hicks believed that there was no difference between all species of animals, humans included. I interpret this belief as oneness and interconnection as seen in Buddhism and Taoism.

After recently inheriting my mother's vintage button collection, I immediately noticed the variety of buttons, each with their differing color, size, shape, material, texture, and decorativeness. However, all of the buttons were kept together in one tin container. As an avid birdwatcher, I regularly use a field guide to help identify different species of birds all of which appear in one book.

Therefore, *A Field Guide to the Button Kingdom* fuses the idea of oneness and diversity while providing the viewer with a contemplative experience focused on paying close attention to the details of each button. The composition of all 484 buttons was determined by a random number generator, and each button was presented equally within the center of a 1" square grid.

> "Let's recognize the unity in diversity and
> the one(ness) in the many." —Lama Surya Das

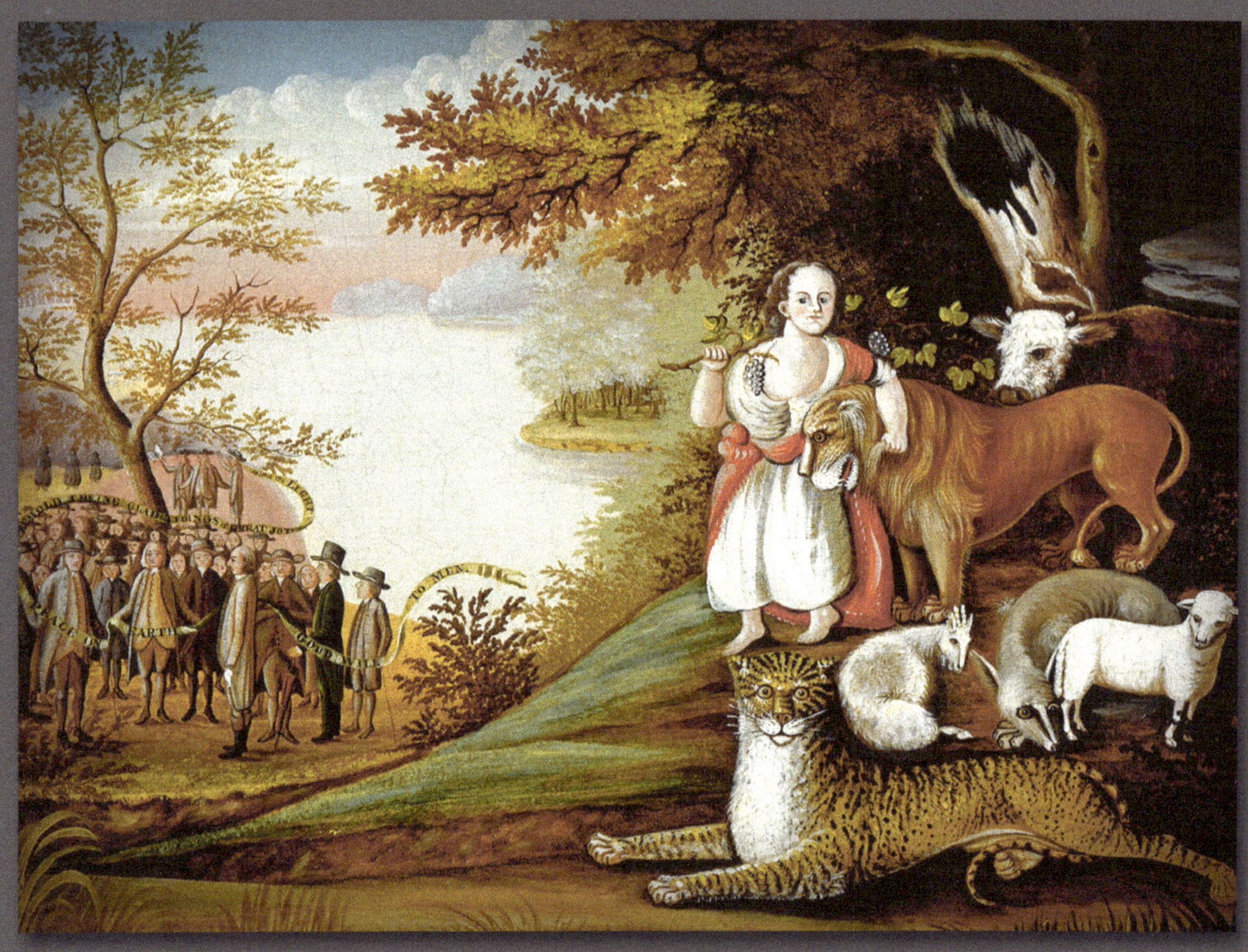

edward hicks
peaceable kingdom (ca. 1830-1832)

Winterthur Museum
Winterthur, Delaware

Patricia Trentacoste

In Conversation

When I heard about Daniel Stewart's *Peaceable Kingdom* book project, I knew immediately, I wanted to interview Pat Custer Denison, a participating Michigan Artists Gallery artist, *and* Edward Hicks himself.

Before I ever met Pat, I knew of her silk-screened, kiln-fired, ceramic-works. They're humorous, bursting with color and they often feature animals enjoying their habitats. For this show, she created three framed graphic prints on paper, 15 editions total, plus two artist's proofs. The poster-style and subject content are deliberate tributes to Hicks' 2-D, folk art.

Hicks himself was a Quaker. Stewardship of the earth is a strong tenet of that religion. Sharing that view, Pat is donating a percentage of the proceeds from her exhibit-sales to Heifer International, a non-profit charity that distributes animals to communities in need.

Getting to Pat's studio/home on the far side of the small, gentle lake we both live on took me down a county road, then up a winding driveway where tribal-looking sculpted mascots pointed the way. I knocked on the door, thinking, *Hicks would love this place*; it's so magical. No answer. I knocked on a different door off a second porch near a quirky monument-garden, and heard rustling from inside. The first door opened and Pat's head popped out cheerily. "You have to knock hard enough to raise the dead. We're under construction." Chip, her carpenter-extraordinaire-husband and facilitator of many of her constructions, including the house and studio, was renovating a room for her photography and giant print-making equipment. It faces out over a reedy wetland around which the lake doglegs and wild life bed down as they please.

I felt a little like Alice through the looking glass, caught between worlds. By then we were indoors, but the wild things were in there with us, including a magnificent parrot named Dandelion—the "photo-bomber" you see in her artworks. Caricatures of critters, both human and animal, grinned at me from decorated cupboards, table-tops, lamp-bases and book-cases. Whimsy, charm and humor, pattern, color and design.

As if that wasn't enough, just beyond the huge menagerie-window, was a leggy, rusty-headed sandhill crane sharing lunch with cat-birds, orioles, squirrels, and white-capped sparrows. Yes, we identified them one by one. Later, the deer would come, and under the stars, the neighborhood black bear. You'll find them all in her creations. Add a koi pond, garden paths, and birdsong. What a wonderland, what a sanctuary. Edward Hicks should come straight over for tea.

However, since Hicks died in 1849, a different method for *his* interview was called for. I decided to extract or paraphrase (anachronize?) his comments from his compiled memoirs and Carolyn J. Weekley's gorgeously illustrated book, *The Kingdoms of Edward Hicks*, published by The Colonial Williamsburg Foundation. Even so, as Pat made clear, Edward Hicks was very much in our midst.

PAT T (INTERVIEWER) **Pat, tell us how you came to be involved with the Peaceable Kingdom exhibit.**

PAT CUSTER DENISON I've always loved Hicks' visual images, his folk art and strong designs. When Sue Ann Rounds kicked off this *art for peace* show based on his work, I was excited.

PAT T **So you already had an admiration for Hicks?**

PAT C D Oh, yes, for years, right from the get-go, you know, his wonderfully designed animals and this very curious story behind how they came about. Do you know that story? What made him finally say, *This is wrong, I just have to be a painter?*

PAT T **I know of it only sketchily. Mr. Hicks, could you elaborate?**

EDWARD HICKS I'm happy to tell thee about it. I was a young teenager when I began my seven-year apprenticeship with a coach-making company as a painter and detailer. During that time, I learned the art of ornamenting ordinary objects by decorating signs, coaches, carriages and furniture. Several Quakers befriended me and were kind enough to house me. Their spirituality impressed me. The "inward light," they believed, could be developed directly, through personal acts of kindness, pacifism, justice. Hierarchies and creeds were not required, equality was. Soon enough, I became a devout Quaker, then a husband, a father, and soon after, a minister.

PAT T **Ah, you had three distinct identities. I imagine they weren't always compatible.**

EDWARD Yes, thou art perceptive and brilliant. I was pulled in opposite directions. You see, my early painting career did not pay well enough to support my family. In part that was because elders from my community disapproved of my artistic style. A true Quaker should produce plainer works. Thinking I would fare better as a farmer, I left my art behind. By then I had five children, but I was no farmer and the debts piled up.

PAT T **And yet, eventually, out of all that strife, came the Peaceable Kingdom series.**

EDWARD Right. Thou art so perceptive, I suspect thou art reading my journal. My ministry took me from Pennsylvania to Niagara Falls. I began doing oil paintings of the countryside. They were plain enough I thought; there were no figures in them. But, my exuberance was censured anyway. This created even more internal spiritual strife for me. Was I an artist? A Quaker? Why couldn't I be both? A schism in the Quaker religion itself occurred over what was and wasn't orthodox. Doing these paintings helped me reconcile those awful tensions and gave me a platform as well. I portrayed wild jungle and farm animals coexisting with children, Indians, Quakers, and political leaders, in idyllic settings. That intense desire to express Quaker quietism in my own language inspired over a hundred peaceable kingdom paintings.

pat custer denison

peaceable kingdom I

fine art print
24" x 30"

There are three prints in my series "The Peaceable Kingdom," after the famous series of 70+ paintings by Edward Hicks (1780 –1849). I am quite skeptical about the sweet notion that prey and predators will ever lie down in peace; still, the chance to do a group of (admittedly rather jittery) animals in such a group was fun.

The story of Edward Hicks painting his heart out and disturbing his Quaker elders by not being "plain" enough has its own appeal. He learned his ornamental trade at 14 years old (highly decorative horse carriages and sign painting). In his 20s he became a Quaker and tried to comply with his elders' stricture that his business was not "plain." He became a farmer, ran into debt and was close to starving his family. When he went back to his painting trade the elders were very unhappy and a schism occurred. Hicks' *Peaceable Kingdom* paintings spoke to his own feelings of peace.

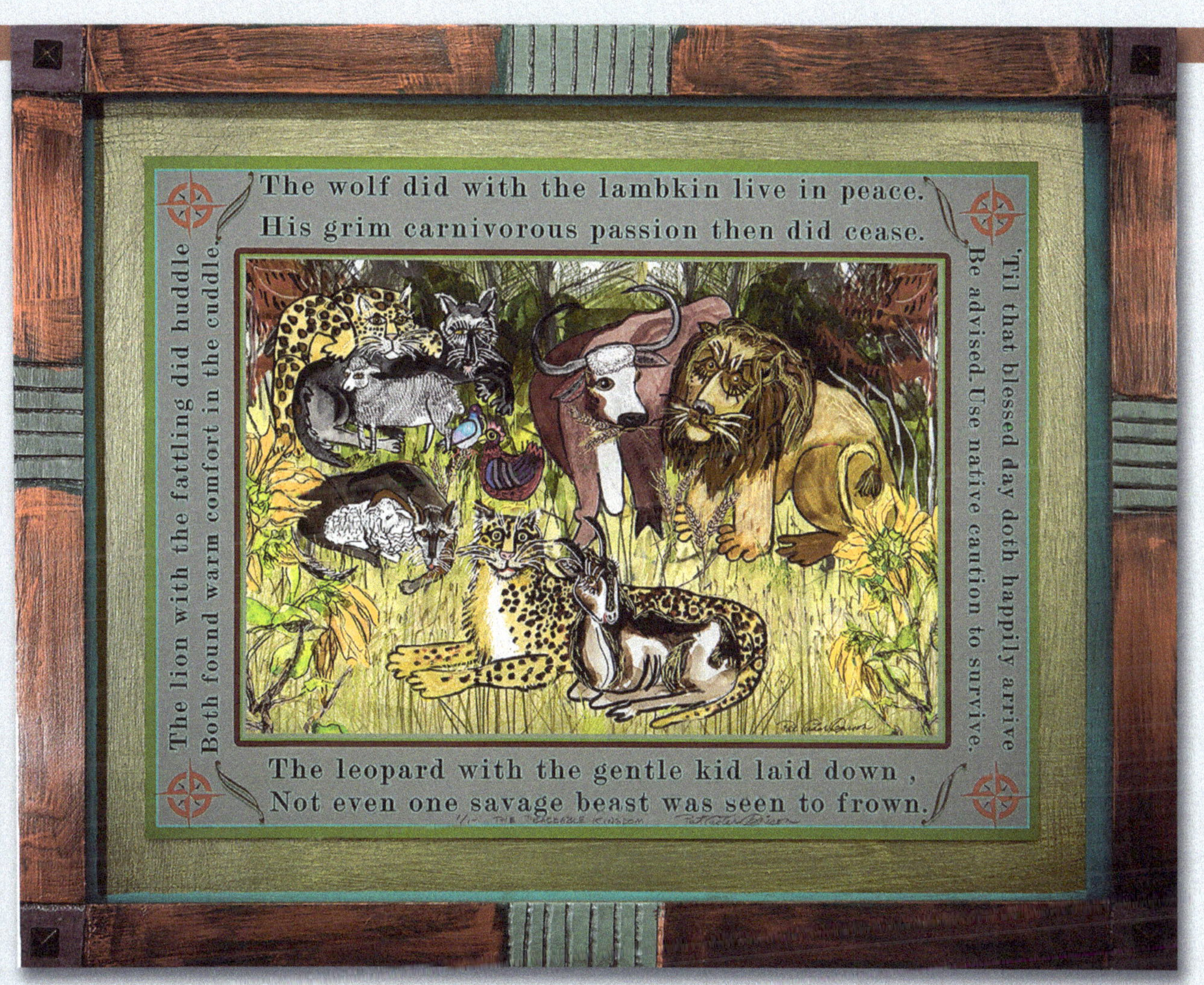

PEACEABLE KINGDOM

PAT T **How perfect, you found a way to be principled, prolific and authentic. It's no wonder you are a revered American folk artist. Pat, I see you nodding your head.**

PAT C D Yes, art was his *trade*. To have your trade devalued is just plain wrong. When I look through all these strange animals in Hicks' paintings, in my own mind, I am sure that consciously or unconsciously, some of his animals look like some of those elders. Their expressions are too human-like.

PAT T **One striking thing about your paintings, Pat, is the way your animals look out from the canvass. Each is a personality-loaded portrait.**

PAT C D I loved that about Hicks' animals as well, and I borrowed a great deal from him for this project. But..., I don't think it would be a good idea for a wolf or a lion to quit being a predator. I'm assuming his creatures' peaceful ways were partly used as illustrations for his sermons.

EDWARD Thee is correct. I often preached by way of metaphor. My animals stood for moral and religious truths. In fact, I deliberately incorporated the four medieval humors: Melancholy (which I symbolized as the wolf), Sanguine (the confident leopard), Phlegmatic, (the imperturbable bear), Choleric (the irascible lion) to emphasize the point that animals can be moody or aggressive. You'll notice the lion eating straw like an ox. That symbolizes my belief that we human animals can and should discipline our natures away from carnivorous impulses toward divine inward light. We can use our moodiness and aggression for the sake of peace.

PAT T **Pat, it's clear that you populated your peaceable kingdoms in a technical way. Will you tell us how you accomplish that?**

PAT C D Gladly. It's a pleasure to be able to talk about my process, but I'll keep it brief. I start with black and white hand-drawings. Then

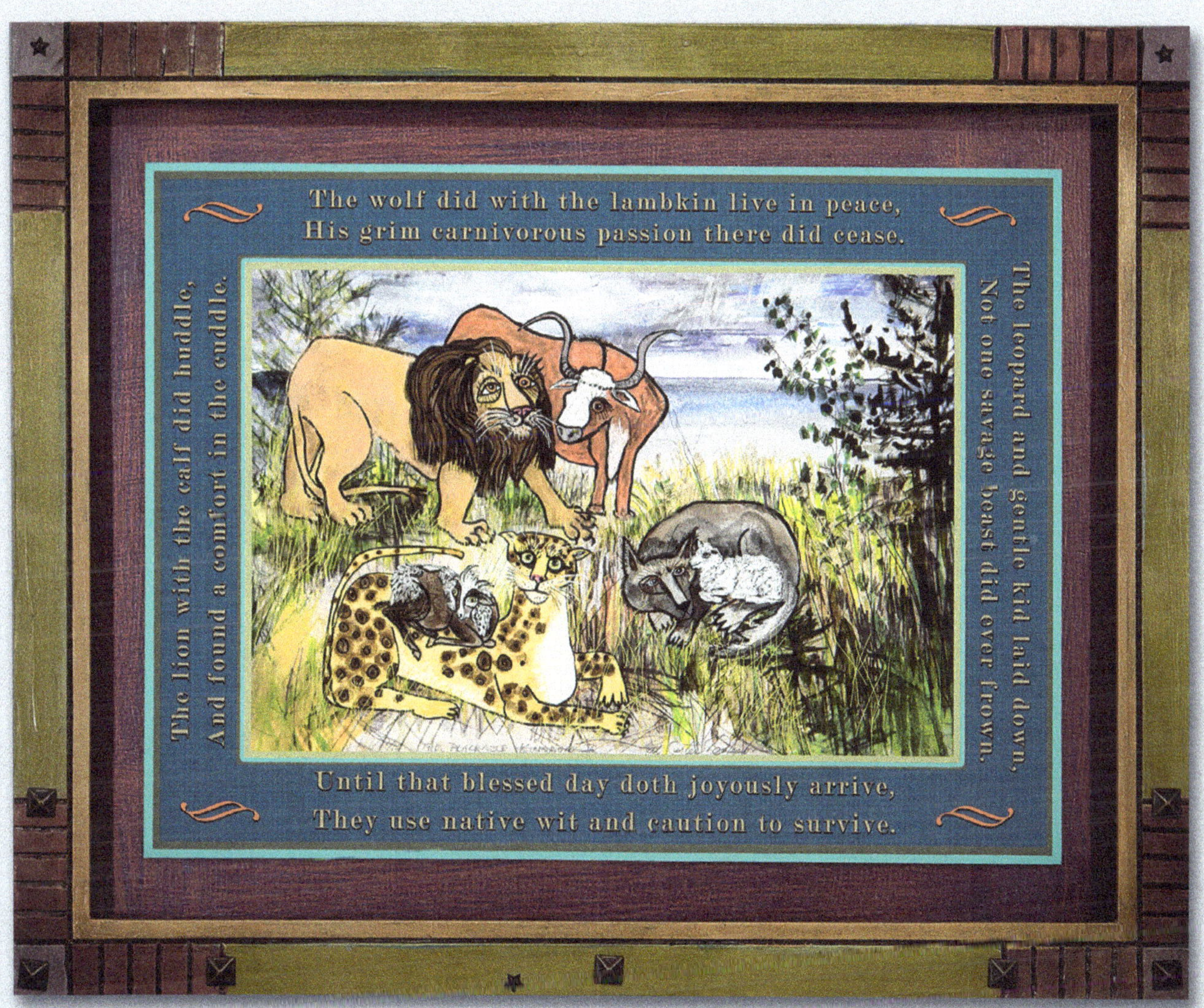

pat custer denison

peaceable kingdom II

fine art print
24″ x 30″

I scan the figures into the computer in layers and make cutouts against transparent backgrounds. I rearrange their placement, then print them out. I apply water colors and rescan that version. I use Photoshop Cloud until I get the image and effect I want. (Here, Pat took me into the other room to show me her giant printer and double-screened computer workspace.) I do dozens, maybe a hundred alterations of hue, scale, composition, etc.

PAT T/EDWARD *(in unison)* **How do you keep track of the changes?**

PAT C D I digitally stack the layers and track each image change in a handwritten notebook.

PAT T **But gee, how do you layer in those equally detailed backgrounds?**

PAT C D I'll show you. (We went into another room to look at dozens of finished watercolors of wetlands, grassy areas, skyscapes, and forests.) I isolate sections of those landscapes and upload them through the process I already told you about. The final prints are collages, but all the elements are my creations. The last thing I do is add highlighting and outlines, borders motifs, that kind of thing, as a final layer of detailing.

PAT T **In a way, the backgrounds are as detailed and prominent as the foregrounds.**

PAT C D It's true. Emphasizing background is part of my style, that flat posterized look, with less dimension and shadowing. Some eyes want to see depth and spatial distance on paper, but I squash my scenes as flat as pancakes. (Here Pat chuckles.) The paper isn't real anyway. You can't walk around on a piece of paper or walk into the distance. I don't create the illusion of receding space. My images are deliberately very busy. If the eyes want to rest, they can look at the wall beyond the picture frame. Assigning hierarchies of aesthetic merit based on approaches to complexity or depth or shadowing doesn't make sense to me. There are many different ways to think about compositions and methods. They're all art.

PAT T **By the way, I think what you do is every bit as complicated as composing a symphony.**

PAT C D Well, thank you. People hear computer art and the mythology comes up, you know, that it's a simple thing, with the machine doing all the work. That's not the case with mine. I carefully monitor and preserve the quality of my prints by using only archival inks and papers.

PAT T **Will you ever go back to non-computer printworks?**

PAT C D Oh, I can do simple hand-paintings that don't require nearly as many decisions about layering. But I get into trouble. I tell myself, "Don't do the black, don't do the black" but the black wants to be done.

PAT T **Like a hijacked-impulse?**

PAT C D Exactly. When doing live painting, mistakes are more difficult to mask-out and accidents become part of the work. I don't believe in perfection. But, I have never had a clear idea of what it is I want to paint. It comes out after I've been working on the piece.

I used to hand-rub my inks onto an etching press, which meant remaking editions over and over. Now, the printer makes my copies, which means I don't have to take in all the ink toxins and get carpal-tunnel for the sake of my art. I don't have to die for my art. The technology is a great help, although I still have to feed and tend it and deal with its nasty tricks.

PAT T **Mr. Hicks told us why he painted animals. Why do *you*? From frogs to bitterns, they show up in nearly all your works.**

PAT C D I think that's just a personal preference. My childhood toys were barnyards. All my bicycles had horse names. My art is filled with creatures.

PAT T **Thank you, Pat. This was grand. We barely touched on all that could be said. I look forward to another chance to do that with you. I think I'll give Edward Hicks the last two**

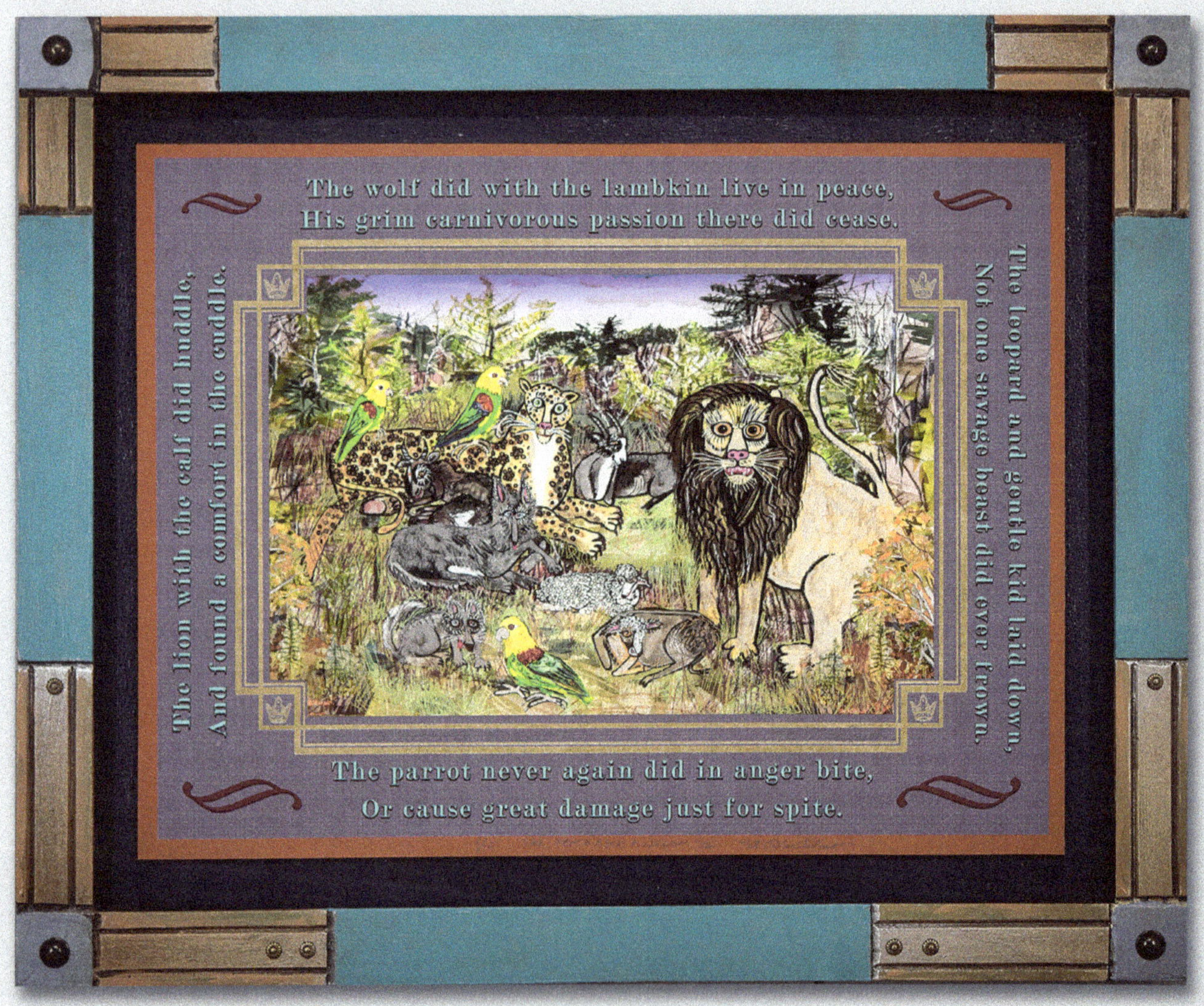

pat custer denison

peaceable kingdom III

fine art print
24″ x 30″

questions. Mr. Hicks, do you have any advice for people who feel melancholy over the state of the world?

EDWARD "The best cure ... is humble industry; what a pity then that they [his closed-minded critics?] would not eat less and work more."

PAT T **And what artistic advice do you have for artists of conscience who value free expression?**

EDWARD I'll tell thee what my lawyer told me, "Edward, thee has now the source of independence within thyself, in thy peculiar talent for painting. Keep to it within the bounds of innocence and usefulness, and thee can always be comfortable."

PAT T **Mr. Hicks, I read that you once described the nation with these words: "Enterprising, aspiring, restless, warlike America."**

EDWARD Yes, thee read correctly.

PAT T **Thank you, Mr. Hicks. Thank you, Pat Custer Denison.**

■

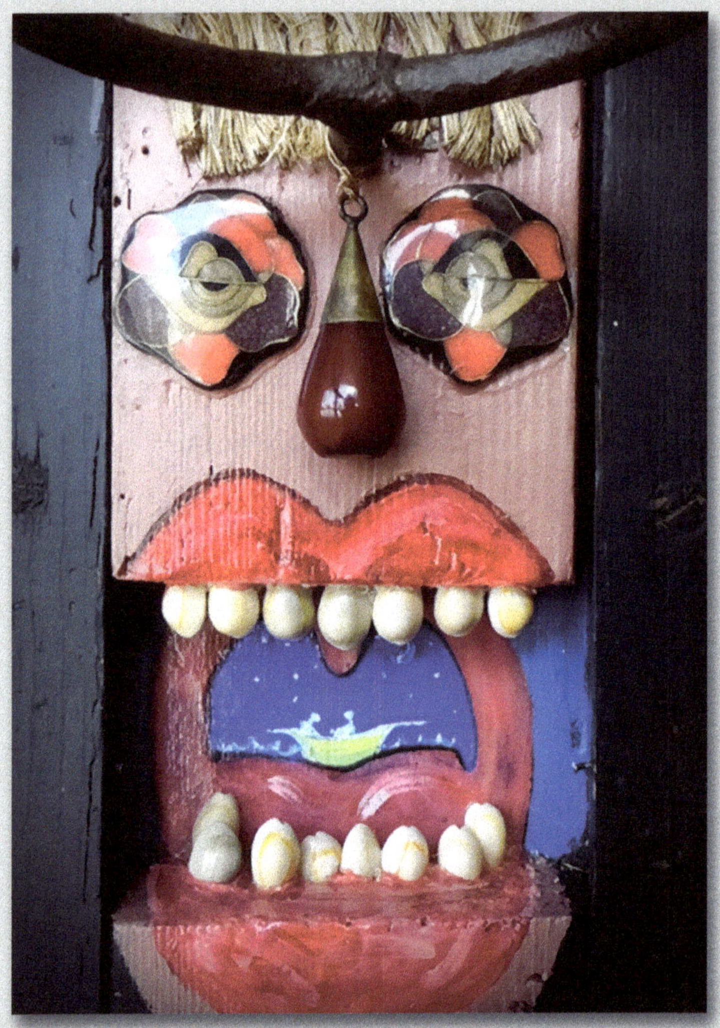

elizabeth paxson

peace dwells within *(detail)*

found objects
36″ tall

I have always been drawn to unusual objects that have a potential for being interactive. This piece grew from an antique object, which may have been used for cutting asparagus. It suggested a face to me, with movable mouth, and metal "horns." I added antique buttons and dangle for the eyes and nose, and cowry shells for teeth. It shows that a peaceful interior (two figures floating serenely in a boat under a starry sky) can dwell inside even a demonic looking character.

Greta Bolger

Disingenuous Guillotine

ARTWORK: *Peace Dwells Within* by Elizabeth Paxson

Your original design was to be useful,
purposeful. True for all of us, I guess,

but the sharpness in your mouth
betrayed you, swelled your lips,

stabbed your hair skyward
swung your nose like a ruddy pendulum,

eyes outsized, faceted like flies. But please.
Asparagus your wooden bellicosity.

Your teeth are fearsome, true, but dull.
Though you look wild and bound up

in contraption, every time you open
your mouth, you reveal yourself a dreamer

floating, befriended, in a flimsy boat,
in love with the untrammeled moon,

the guileless stars, sailing open-hearted
toward the peaceable kingdom
while it may yet be found.

Daniel Stewart

Dominion

The scream pulls me from sleep. I spend a moment caught in between sleeping and waking, until the world around me resolves in pieces: window; bed; body; clock. It's 5:30—still deep within the November night. I'm in bed. I'm alone.

I'm surprised less by being awake than by being asleep beforehand. It's been an unsettled, restless night. My wife, Amanda, slipped out of bed hours ago. She must be on the couch downstairs, where we often retreat when we're sleepless to keep from waking up the other. But the scream probably woke her up, too.

It was the sound of a cat, the kind of screech that punctuates an animal skirmish. Probably it was our outdoor cat, who arrived uninvited a couple of years ago and began patrolling our farmhouse, barn and outbuildings; eventually we named her Alice. We haven't let her inside, though, because Alice is aggressive toward other cats and we already had an indoor cat, Jenks; sometimes Alice takes a high perch and stares in at Jenks through the windows, her eyes fierce and covetous.

A few days ago we noticed an unfamiliar cat skirting the edges of the cedars that separate our house from the road, so I'm not surprised by the trouble. It's quiet again—fights like these are usually quick—but I slip from beneath the twisted sheets and dress without turning on any lights. I'll just go outside, as quietly as I can, and make sure everything is alright. The stairs creak as I pad my way down.

Before I went to bed I saw Alice sleeping in a chair on our front porch. It's cool for sleeping outside. We have a shelter for her in the garage, a squat, oversize wood box with an open doorway and Plexiglas window, plus insulated walls and a heating pad, but Alice has never much cared for it. Maybe it feels cramped. Maybe she feels unsafe in a tiny house with just a single exit. She uses it when she must, so although it's northern Michigan in autumn, there's still time before the bitter cold will come.

On the few steps from the stairs to the porch door I pass the doorway into the living room. The shadow that must be Amanda is unmoving on the couch, but Jenks has been awakened by the sound, just like me. I thought he'd be on a window ledge, looking outside, but instead he's on the floor, his ears turned alertly toward the window. I open the door to the porch, then the storm door, trying to be quiet.

I pull from my pocket the small flashlight I usually keep there. We live on an unlighted, headlight-swallowing country road, and in autumn each night is longer than the one before it. If the clouds block out light from the moon and stars, the encompassing darkness makes it hard even to see the boundary between the earth and the sky—shadow from black. The floodlight mounted beside the back door seems bright, but it does little to pierce the unsettling dark. The cool, hard metal cylinder in my pocket reassures me that I can find my way in that darkness. It makes me feel safe.

Alice is not on the chair. I turn on the flashlight and begin to sweep its beam into the night. The vast night reminds me how small she is. She's a calico, and when I see her at night, the third of her fur that is raven-black melts into the long shadows. When she's awake she vibrates with energy, but what seems bold under the sun can seem like foolhardiness beneath the stars.

Looking for animals at night is mostly about watching for the reflections of nocturnal eyes, and the hard white beam of my light catches a pair of eyes. They're blue-green but vanish instantly, and the gray outline around them shrinks back into the shadows without making a sound. Most creatures stare back at lights, but not this one.

Then I see the brown, black and white patches of Alice's back. She's stretched out full-length on the ground, near the base of the old maple. It takes several long moments—longer than it should—before I realize Alice is dead. It takes still another moment before I realize I heard her die.

I turn off my flashlight and kneel beside her. In the gray dimness she looks unmarked, except for a ruffling of fur around her face. I can see the dark tip of her tongue, extended just beyond the teeth of her half-open mouth. When I touch her, she feels as she has always felt, soft and warm. Still warm.

I need to wrap her. There are towels near the washing machine—old, frayed towels, retired from use. I try to keep the storm door from slamming behind me.

"What happened?" Amanda asks. She's still curled onto the couch, her voice no more than half awake.

"Alice is dead," I say.

Amanda begins to sob. I don't know why I said it that way, without preamble or softening. I know it was too abrupt, too harsh even as the words left my mouth, but only a part of my brain seems to be working.

I pick up the first towel I find that seems large enough, a pink towel with threads hanging from its frayed edges. Amanda comes back outside with me, to Alice.

"Don't turn on the light," Amanda says, and I don't. She touches Alice, too.

Then I put the towel over Alice and lift her up, wrapping the rough cotton around her. I won't be able to bury her until sunrise, so I'll put her in the back of my car until then. She seems heavier than she was when she was alive.

When I close the hatch the car's dome lights remain on for many seconds, before finally blinking out. We stand as the darkness envelops us, letting our eyes readjust. It's a clear, moonless night; the winds are still. We look up, watching the shimmer of the remote stars. Amanda points: one of the stars is moving, but at a stately pace—a satellite, or maybe the space station. Then I see another star carving its own straight line across the black, its path at a sharp angle to the first.

The sunrise seems impossibly distant but there's no hope to return to sleep. Behind the beam of my flashlight I wander to the front of the house, to where I found Alice. I play the light across the yard again—and this time I see him, just at the edge of the beam. He avoids looking at my light so I see no details, just the gray, almost featureless outline. The coyote stands motionless for just a moment, then in a quick but unhurried motion slips again into the shelter of the cedars.

"HE WAS COMING BACK FOR HER BODY," I SAY TO A CAT-LOVING FRIEND several days later.

"Did you shoot it?" she replies.

I'm taken aback. We inherited a .22 rifle with the house, but I keep it in a closet; I don't know where the ammunition clip is. "I didn't even think of that," I say.

She shakes her head in disappointment and disapproval. "They'll keep coming back until they get all the cats in the neighborhood."

This sounds true enough. We have another visiting cat, a feral tom who for years had been appearing every now and again around the barn, always at a distance. But one day he surprised us by rubbing against Amanda's leg, and he'd even begun allowing a little petting. I put out enough cat food for him, too, and a bed. He ignored Alice's protests and became a frequent visitor, and sometimes even a daily one. We began calling him Blue, for the inkiness of his unbroken blue-black fur.

But we hadn't seen Blue in several days and, as it turned out, would never see him again.

I don't tell my friend what I felt after watching the coyote retreat into the darkness. The regret about what I had not done had nothing to do with rifles.

We live in the country, and while we have neighbors I think it is not exactly a neighborhood. I think I cannot claim more dominion over this land than can the coyotes. I walk outside in the daylight and mow grass, trim trees, pull weeds and plant and water seedlings. When the twilight comes, though, I quiet the pounding engines, put away the wood and steel tools, and retreat inside. Sometimes, from that dark world beyond my small compass of artificial light, I hear the echoing howls and frantic yips of the coyotes. The night is an alien place. Its rules are different.

I thought Alice, herself a fearsome hunter, was too clever and too quick to be hunted. I was wrong, but I felt toward the coyote nothing like

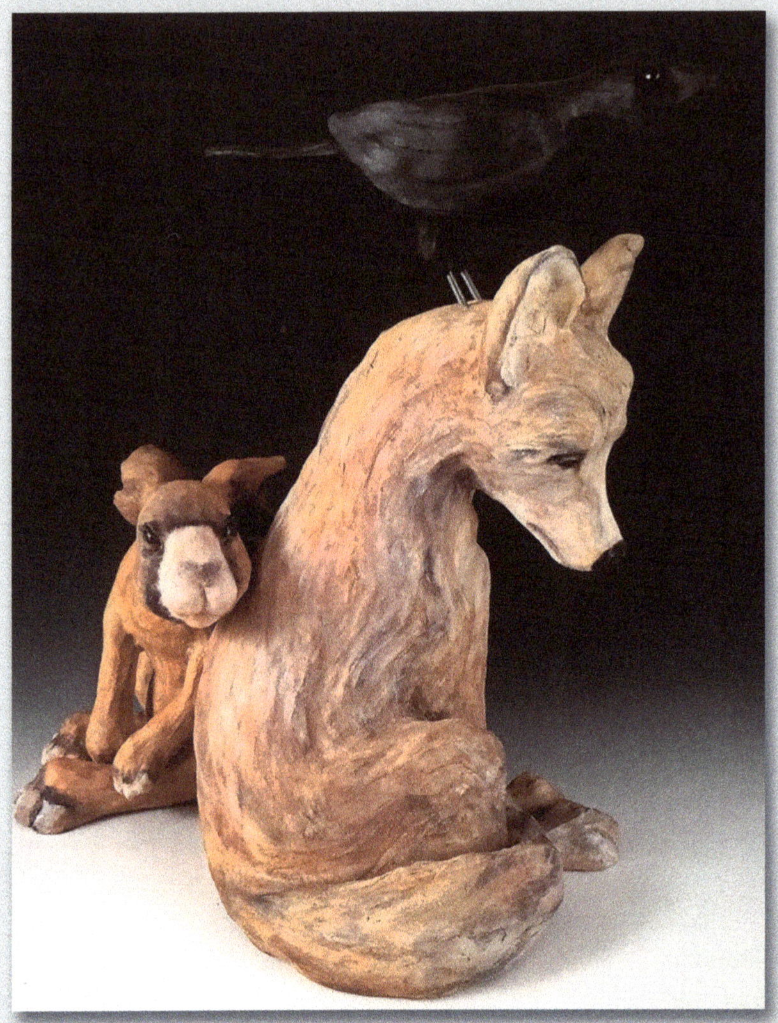

julie kradel
community

ceramic
21″ x 18″

A peaceable kingdom begins with the community that we live in. In my community there are the residents who have lived there before me/us, the crows, the rabbits, the coyotes. We, the humans, rage war upon them daily, as we feel they are encroaching on us. A true Peaceable Kingdom for the community, as well as our world, would be understanding and accepting of who each of us are. Through that, we can come together in harmony and in peace.

anger or fear—or affection. I felt instead that I had glimpsed the edge of a vast mystery, an opening to a world I could not understand. I could see its outline but not its import. I had heard death come, but I think cat and coyote—each of them both hunter and hunted—shared an understanding of something that was beyond me.

I had seen Alice hunt, and our barn cat before her, too. I had seen their prey—chipmunks and mice mostly—struggle in their desperation to escape. I had seen them fight for their lives to the end—or, rather, to just before the end. Sometimes the struggle stopped not at death, but at the far edge of life. I don't know if it was an acceptance of death, but maybe it was a kind of recognition. Sometimes at the end there was a moment of stillness. The killing bite came without rancor, as well as without pity.

Some time after I watched the coyote slip away, I wondered if I had somehow broken the compact between predator and prey. The coyote had hunted, and hunted well, and still was hungry.

The cold, blue-white light of my flashlight illuminated no answers to the mystery. It had shown me only a gray outline. It might have been a ghost, or the shadow of the trickster who appears in so many Native American legends.

A few years ago a dog-owning friend was warned by his veterinarian about letting their golden retriever stray from his house with coyotes in the neighborhood. Coyotes were clever in luring domestic dogs to their deaths, he was told.

"But she's a big dog," he protested. "She's much bigger than a coyote. Wouldn't that keep her safe?"

The veterinarian paused to give him a sober look, then said, emphasizing each syllable, "*Wild always wins.*"

In the wild of the dark right outside my door, the coyote had somehow tricked Alice into bolting for a refuge she could not reach. Alice could climb almost as quickly as a squirrel. I found her on the roots of the maple tree; she would have been safe up in its branches.

§ § §

THE HOLE I'M DIGGING IS TOO BIG. I'M DIGGING INTO THE HILLSIDE behind the house, amid the copse of oak, maple and beech trees my father-in-law planted; now they're tall and he's gone. The hill is sandy, and except for some tree roots and clutching undergrowth, the digging is almost easy. I dig down a foot, then two, then deeper still on the uphill side to flatten the bottom of the hole. I want it to be deep enough that no scavenger will disturb it. I'm tired of digging, but this has less to do with the digging than with the other graves. This is the fourth hole I've dug on this hillside—my father-in-law's dog and now a third cat, only one of whom died in old age. I'm tired of burying pets.

The hole is almost three feet across now, surrounded by dirt and clumps of sod, when I finally stop and stick the shovel blade-first into the ground. I call for Amanda, then go to the car and open the hatch. I pick up Alice and carry her, still wrapped in the towel, back up the hill. She's cold now, and stiff.

Before I place Alice into the ground, Amanda peels back a little of the towel. Her fur is still soft, but untidy. I try to smooth her side, but to little use. What will happen has already begun.

SOMETIMES, COYOTE IS MORE THAN A TRICKSTER. THERE'S A STORY TOLD among the Caddo nations, who lived along the banks of the Red River in the southern Great Plains. In the beginning, says the tale, there was no death. In time, however, the earth began to overflow with humanity. Soon there would not be enough food.

At a council to discuss the problem, the men proposed that people should die—but only for a little while. For men to die forever, they said, would lead to so much grief that it would drive all happiness from the world. So the council decided that when men died, the medicine men would build a grass house, facing East, and there sing a song to draw the spirit into the house. The spirit's arrival would restore the man to life.

But Coyote had come to the council, too, and he knew this plan was no answer to the problem. He argued his point, but the men would not agree to Coyote's undeniable, unbearable logic.

When the first man died, the medicine men went to the grass house as planned, and they began to sing the song to call the spirit. After ten days the spirit appeared, carried in a whirlwind from the West. But as the whirlwind was about to reach the house, Coyote slammed the door shut. The spirit passed on with the wind, forever.

In that way, says the tale, Coyote made death permanent, and in our grief and in our rage, we have been chasing him ever since.

I KEEP PACKING MORE DIRT AROUND THE GRAVE. I'VE COVERED IT AGAIN with the sod I removed, but it's a mound now and the sod doesn't cover it completely. I scoop more dirt around the edges and pack it down, and scoop and pack.

Finally Amanda touches me on the back. "It'll settle," she says, and of course she's right. I pack the dirt a little more, then stand up, brushing dirt from my pants.

This is a rocky landscape, and for more than a hundred years men have been making little cairns of unearthed rocks. From one of the piles Amanda has found a suitable heavy stone. I place it on top of the fresh mound, laying it down gently, as if the gentleness matters. "We'll miss you, Alice," I say.

And then we walk down the hill and I put the shovels back into the garage and we turn to the plans and schedules and responsibilities we had planned for the day, just a little bit late.

Alice understood death better than I ever will. But this part, what takes place on the hillside after, is something I think only we can know.

■

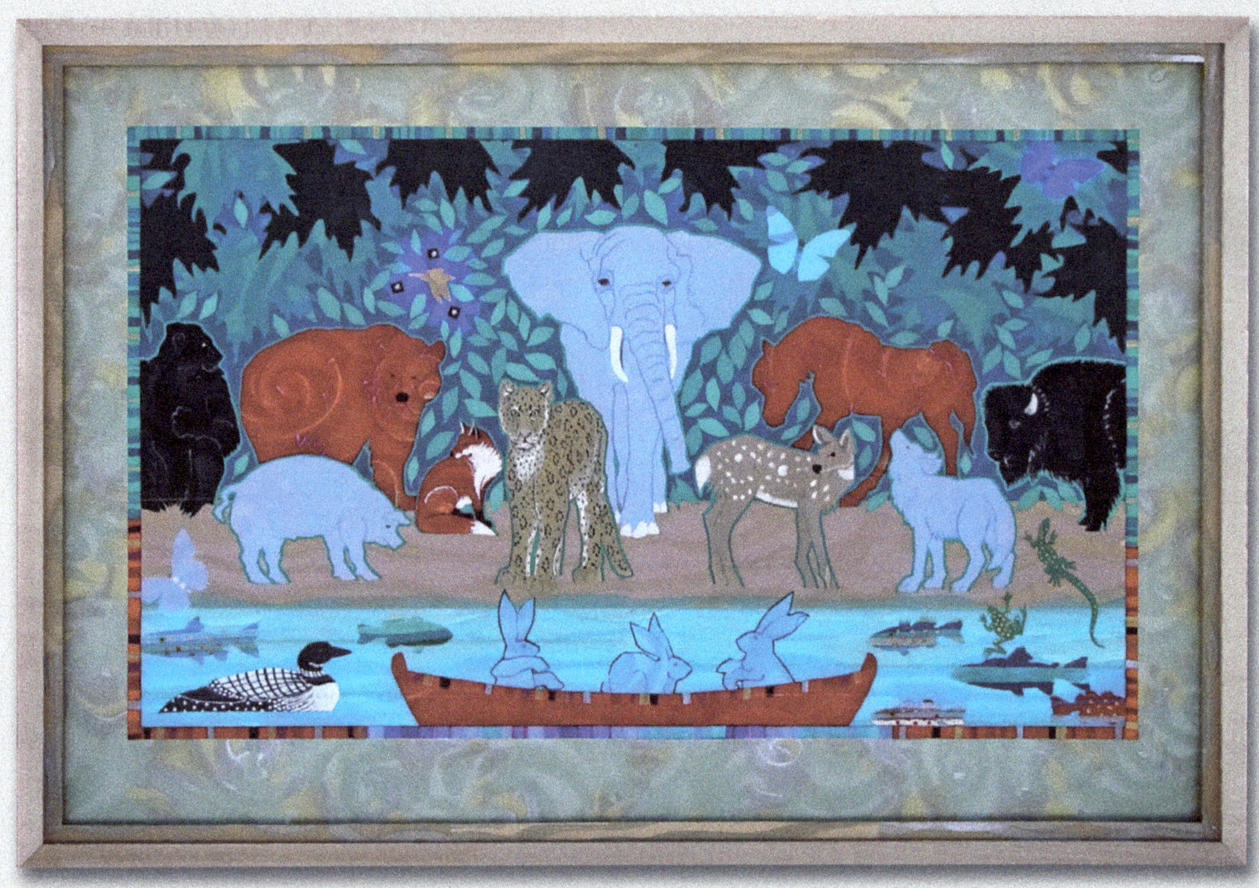

char bickel

peaceable kingdom

silk screen collage
25″ x 37″

Edward Hicks' *Peaceable Kingdom* paintings encourage me to think about my own animal nature, with all of its complexity. I feel that the animals in the paintings are personified by us. But then they also animalize us with their glorious, rich variety of forms. What happens to them happens also to us.

Catherine Turnbull

Peaceable Kingdom

Well,
what if nobody ate anybody
anymore? I mean, you look
at these Edward Hicks—
the tigers and lions with people-eyes,
the little child's stiff arm over a predator
like the animal is a crutch,
and the stark levels of earth dividing everything
into something crowded and moving,
and William Penn so often in the background
circled by natives, signing the document
this Quaker painter admired so much
he put a banner around the scene sometimes,
Mind the light within, it is a glad tiding,
there's nothing more Quaker than that idea,
those lions looking out at us with such astonishment
to be next to an ox and not stalking it,
I see the point, I see the lion and the ox sharing
the same stalk of grain, but *come on,*
it would never work. The world in no time
infested with uneaten insects, uneaten fish.
The lamb and the ibex have to lie down
into their fate like the grasses before them.
And nobody wants a little child
out in front, that's for damn sure.

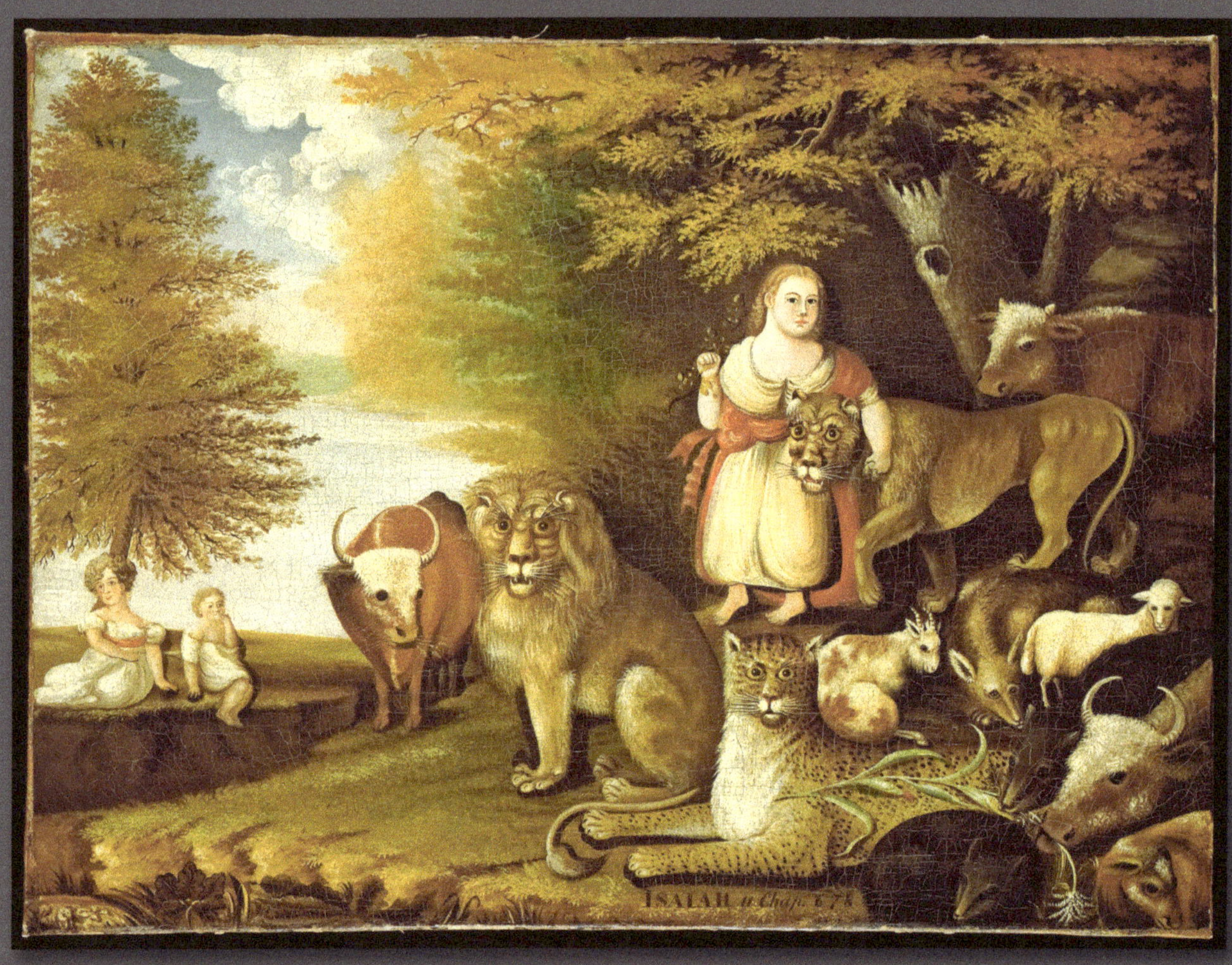

edward hicks
peaceable kingdom (1833)

Worcester Art Museum
Worcester, Massachusetts

Alice Hansen

Edward Hicks Symphony

Edward Hicks' painting is a visual symphony depicting hope for peace in the world. The music begins quietly with the violins and moves around the orchestra until all musicians with their instruments are included in a loud but harmonious sound. It becomes light to reflect the crowd of people on the side and continues light perhaps even staccato changing between the instruments and concludes once again with all instrumentation.

The second movement is strong with an emphasis on drums and plodding trombones and bassoons—and is slow so it's felt deep in the soul.

The third movement reflects children and their innate care and love for all kinds of animals and humans. This would be portrayed by violins, harps and wind instruments mainly flutes and oboes. It would be flighty and all over the place but grounded by the clarinets—with snare drums and the rest of the percussion section.

The fourth and last movement would return to the first movement but utilizing stronger music with heavy percussion, trumpets and horns—ending in a crescendo.

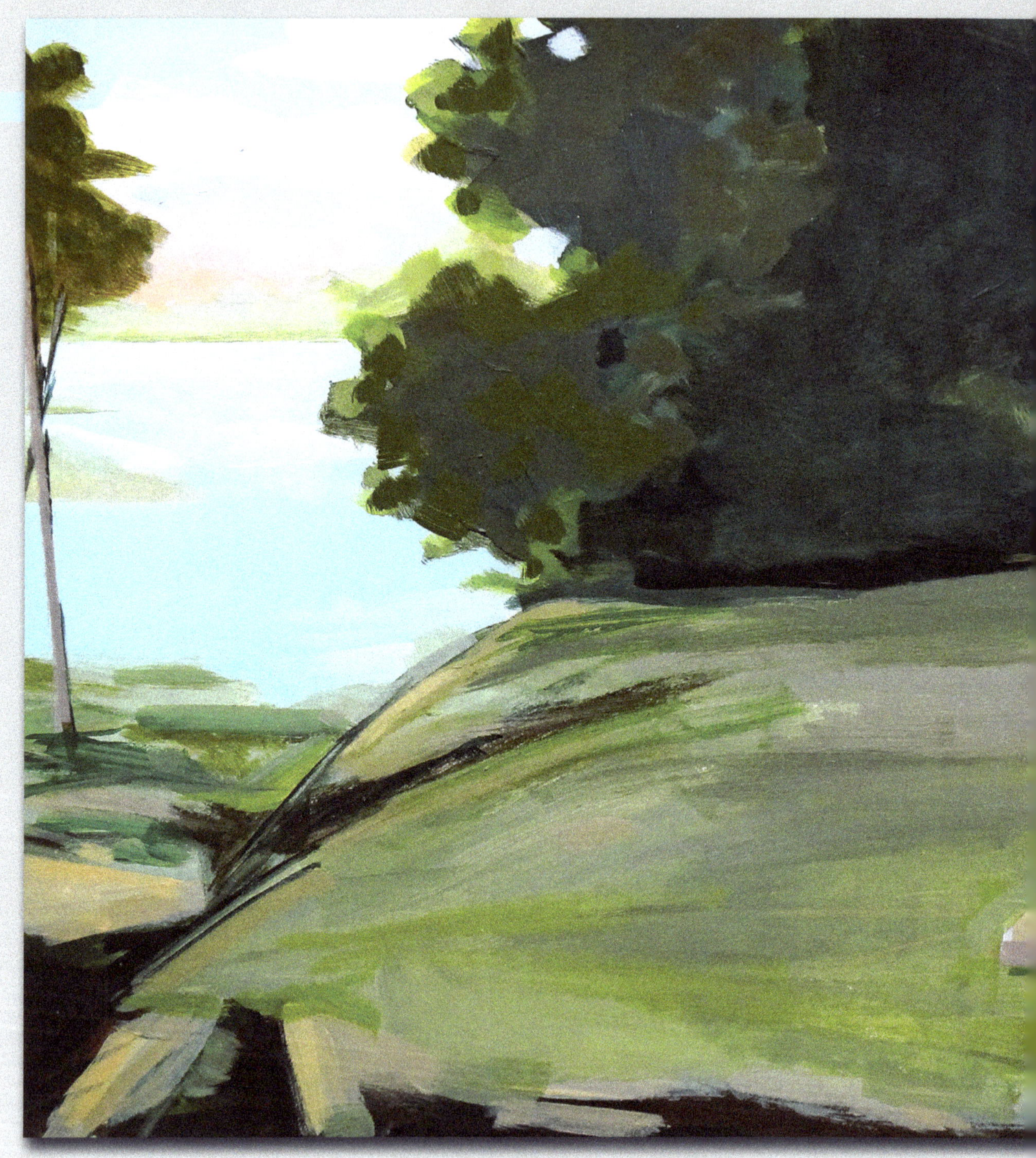

joan richmond
only the lambs

casein on paper
15″ x 17″

This image, inspired by Edward Hicks' *The Peaceable Kingdom* (one of his 62 versions), reconstructs the landscape of his painting, but then only includes the lambs to represent the animals. No human characters are included. The question is then asked, *Can only the lambs provide a peaceable kingdom?*

Anne-Marie Oomen

Sans

inspired by "Only the Lambs" by Joan Richmond

Imagine the land
with only the lambs.

Imagine the land
sans lions, leopards, bears,

sans predators and prey,
treaties broken, verses clichéd.

Imagine the land
with only that green, grassy

hillside—not even
one messianic child in white.

Imagine the land at last
empty but for lambs.

That peace,
that quiet.

Betsy Emdin

Peaceable Kingdom

"P" was one of my favorite volumes of the *World Book Encyclopedia* because it contained the section on painting. Pages and pages were devoted to reproductions of paintings from antiquity to the near present which was circa 1962 when we acquired the set. I'd pull "P" out from the bookshelf in the living room, curl up in the chair under the shelf and peruse the art. It was a paper museum I wandered along; a private party for an only child. There were Giotto's anguished angels mourning the crucified Christ in *Lamentation*, although I don't know if I yet knew what that word meant. The angels' emotion, their contorted faces were so different than the subdued Protestantism in which I was steeped. My mother didn't pore over the encyclopedias like I did, but I suspected she wouldn't care for Giotto's work.

There was a painting of a tornado (*Tornado Over Kansas* by John Steuart Curry) that looked just like a scene from *The Wizard of Oz*. It gave me chills. Hopper's *Early Sunday Morning*, with brick facades of buildings that reminded me of the main streets Grand Haven and Holland, Michigan, small towns where we took Saturday afternoon drives with my grandma. Stories spun in my head of the people who slept in the apartments above the stores. They might not be the sort who would get up and go to church.

And there was the *Peaceable Kingdom*. It was like a storybook illustration. A picture that could be hung on my bedroom wall, not like the gilded wall hangings and furniture store landscapes that decorated the living room walls of my house. Bright color. Leopards, lions, lambs. Beasts with giant horns. Gathered in an unlikely flock, posed, but so alive in their expression. Inquisitive. These animals had spirit. A Sunday School lesson come to life.

The leopard in repose looked right at the viewer—at me. I liked all the big cats, and leopards were my favorite. In my third-grade class photo my winter jacket is visible in the background, hung on a hook in my cubby. It was plush fur with black spots—like the cat in the painting. I loved that coat. It was my first animal print garment in an era when little girls wore pastels or plaid dresses, and if my mother had her way, the dress would have a white color and cuffs. Wild animal prints were worn by wild women. Even I knew that at my tender age. Floozies. Hussies. Women that my mother didn't approve of. They were not worn by children. But I loved wild cats, in clothing or pictures. And I was captivated by the cat with curious eyes looking out from his peaceable kingdom and so different from the animals I watched on *Wild Kingdom*. Big eyes, relaxed amongst fellow creatures while a few cherubic children cavorted amongst them. If I was there I could nuzzle the lion's mane, touch the horn of the ox, and pet the gorgeous leopard who gazed at me.

I'd scrutinized the painting many times before I realized there were people in the background. Men who looked like the man on the Quaker Oats box, and Indians. Boys played cowboys and Indians with cap guns and rubber tomahawks. My cousins had plastic figures of cowboys and Indians that warred with one another. My father watched westerns on TV where Indians were clad in leather and feathers and shot bow and arrows while cowboys in vests and Stetsons fired back with rifles. In play and entertainment we thought Indians were the enemy. In the painting it looked like Quakers and the Indians were friends. Did I read it in the "Q" volume, or did my mom explain that Quakers were a religion of peace? They wouldn't fight the Indians. But in the painting, the doings of the people were background.

The animals were the focus. Leopards and kids, lions and lambs lying down together. I knew this was in the Bible. The way the world was supposed to be but wasn't. There was Russia and Atomic bombs. Negroes being beaten up for civil rights. Horrifying photos of Buddhist monks burning themselves alive for something I didn't understand. Something about war. The painting was about a someday world, the promise of my Sunday School lessons. A promise not yet fulfilled.

More than fifty years later we still wait. Planet earth spins on. We still need to prove that Black Lives Matter. Religious divisiveness still incites war. And there is still Russia. My soul succumbs to the undertow of turmoil. I remind myself to seek the contentment I found as a child curled up with an encyclopedia. The 2018 edition of the *World Book Encyclopedia* no longer has the *Peaceable Kingdom* in the P volume. It is now under F, for Folk Art, and is a different version that what was in my family's set. But what astonished me most was that the *World Book* still existed in a hardbound edition. That made me happy. The art in its 1962 version opened my eyes to vision, creativity, and all that can be done with a single idea.

Over the years I've acquired a wardrobe full of animal prints and a spotted jacket still hangs in my entry. Though I'd love a world where I could stroke a leopard and cuddle a wolf, I'm content with snuggling with my dog and cat upon a zebra striped bedspread in our own Peaceable Queendom.

■

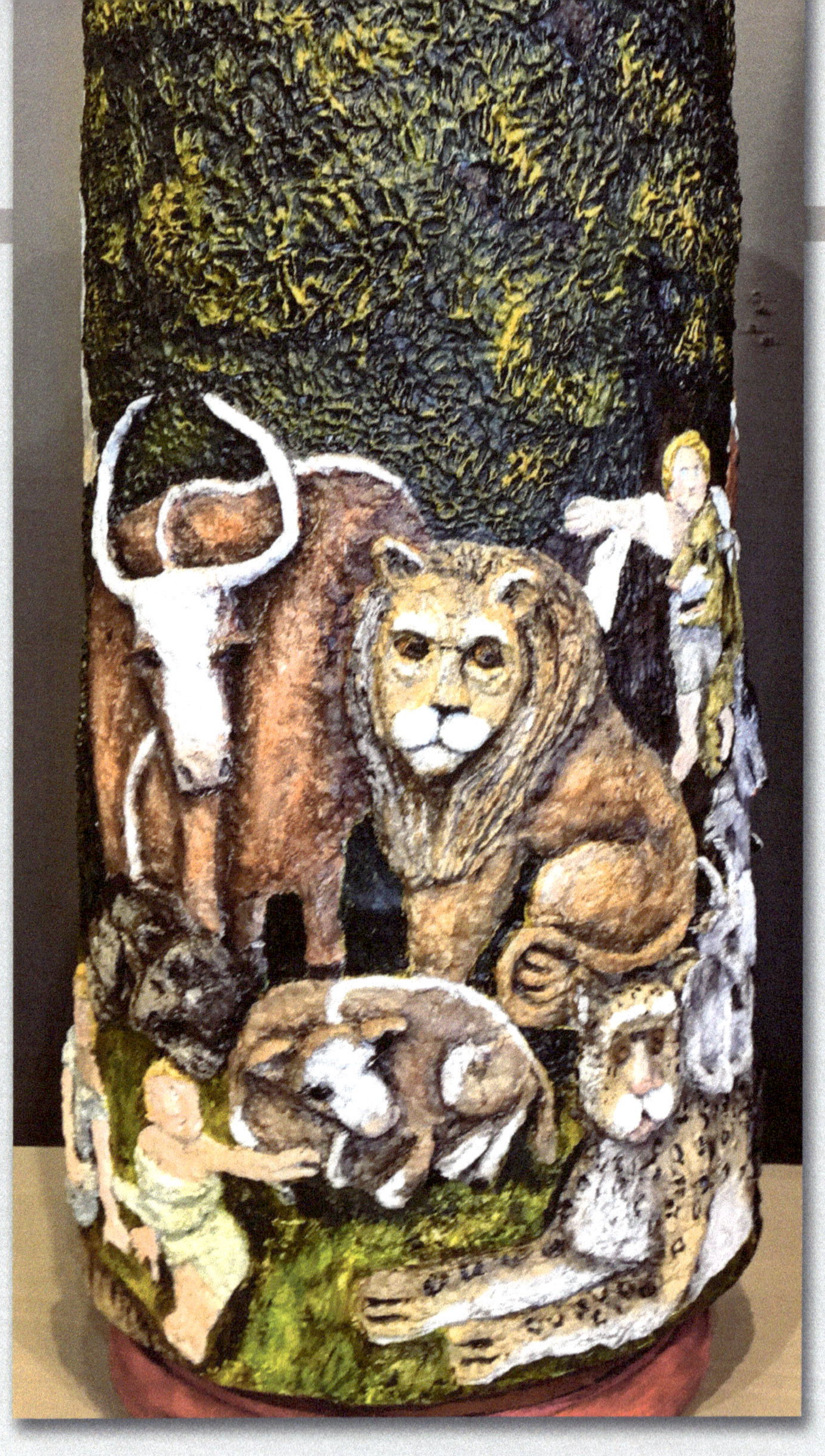

johnna langen
prayer for a peaceable kingdom
prayer wheel *(detail)*

paper clay scultpure/mixed media
22″ x 8″

With my artwork, I enjoy creating—trees, animals, and objects that seem to be pulled from the illustrated pages of a children's book and brought to life with sculptural dimension and some level of movement. Edward Hicks' painting, *Peaceable Kingdom*, with his unique perspective and stylized animals, gives me a great foundation of ideas for my inspiration. In *Prayer for a Peaceable Kingdom* I use my recycled mail to make paper clay with which I create a prayer wheel. As a mixed media artist I think this particular medium seems to represent the same cycle of connectedness and becoming in which I capture my own prayer for peace. The animals want to come to life, to lift themselves from their painted acrylic moorings and they show us people how to do it—this peace thing, if we would only pay attention.

In *Prayer for a Peaceable Kingdom* I seek to take Hicks' painting and move it from a static linear piece with edges and boundaries, to one of sculpture without beginning or end that wishes to breathe the prayer of peace into the kingdom that Hicks once imagined, by using the model of the Tibetan prayer wheel. When spinning the wheel, with its contained prayers, the Tibetan Buddhists believe the movement gives energy to the words contained inside, from prayer to praying. In this same way, I have created a physical prayer container in which one can contain different prayers, from many people, so that just one person can pray for the lot of us with a simple spin of the wheel. A prayer for a Peaceable Kingdom, Hicks' kingdom, our kingdom—God's Kingdom of nature, beast, and man.

Alison Arthur

Prayer Wheel

Layer upon layer
prayer upon prayer
words tumble,
alphabet of good intentions
spun into a soup.

This prayer wheel
from repurposed paper
wraps cylinder.
Recycled news numbs
as culture pleads for justice.

Rearranged letters form
hateful words flung
from body cage, a tornado.
Shattering connections,
patient prospects for peace
squelched by impulsive action.

Humans fear what
we don't understand.
Like a prayer wheel,
hope buried inside
domain not soulless.

Prayers for peace feel unanswered.
Words walk through us,
help make sense of the world.
Wind whipped prayer flags
churn namaste into air.
Sacred texts expose
ancient wisdom,
our better selves.

Trail of tangled blessings
hopeful to connect
prayer wheel and inner spirit
behold peaceable realm.

Elizabeth Paxson

The Light of Tongues

> If we give you a pistol, will you fight for the Lord?
> But you can't kill the devil with a gun or a sword.
> Will you swear on the Bible? "I will not!" said he,
> "for the truth is more holy than the book to me."
>
> — From "Walk in the Light" (or "The George Fox Song")
> by Sydney Carter (1964)

Let creatures speak
through tongues once wild
that tasted flesh
now tamed by love,
lie down like pups
beside the child.

Truth is a tongue on fire with light
it licks the liar and the cheat,
peels away pretense and pride
leaving raw the flesh of fools
who, once disarmed
kneel in defeat.

Let brothers make
no angry sounds
let sweetened tongues
abide with peace,
in nature's grace
may love abound;

all weapons down
all weapons down.

> Your holy hearsay is not evidence, Give me the good news in the present tense… So shut the Bible up and show me how The Christ you talk about is living now."
>
> — Sydney Carter (1915-2004)

Sydney Carter was the author of songs, both "Lord of the Dance" and "Walk in the Light," also known as "The George Fox Song." Though not a Quaker, he was a British pacifist and served in the ambulance corps during World War II.

Artist and Quaker preacher Edward Hicks remained true to the original tenants of the Quaker faith.

In the 1820s, Hicks was involved in the great dispute within the Quakers. "Orthodox" members favored reading the bible and rigid social conformity. He sided with his cousin, Elias Hicks, who stressed a more intense spirituality and reliance on the "inner light" of the original sect's teachings.

The full lyrics of Carter's song "Walk in the Light," written in 1964, emphasize this belief in truth over orthodoxy.

There's a light that is shining in the heart of man
It's the light that was shining when the world began
There's a light that is shining in the Turk and the Jew
There's a light that is shining, friend, in me and you.

Chorus:
Walk in the Light, wherever you may be
Walk in the Light, wherever you may be
With my old leather breeches and my shaggy, shaggy locks
I am walking in the glory of the Light, said Fox.

With a book and a steeple and a bell and a key
Well they'll bind you forever, but they can't, said he
For the book it will perish and the steeple will fall
And the light will be shining at the end of it all.

Chorus

If we give you a pistol, will you fight for the Lord?
But you can't kill the devil with a gun or a sword.
Will you swear on the Bible? "I will not!" said he,
"For the Truth is more holy than the book to me."

Chorus

There's an ocean of darkness and I drown in the night
Till I come through the darkness to the ocean of Light
And the Light is forever, and the Light it is free
And I walk in the glory of the Light, said he.

Chorus

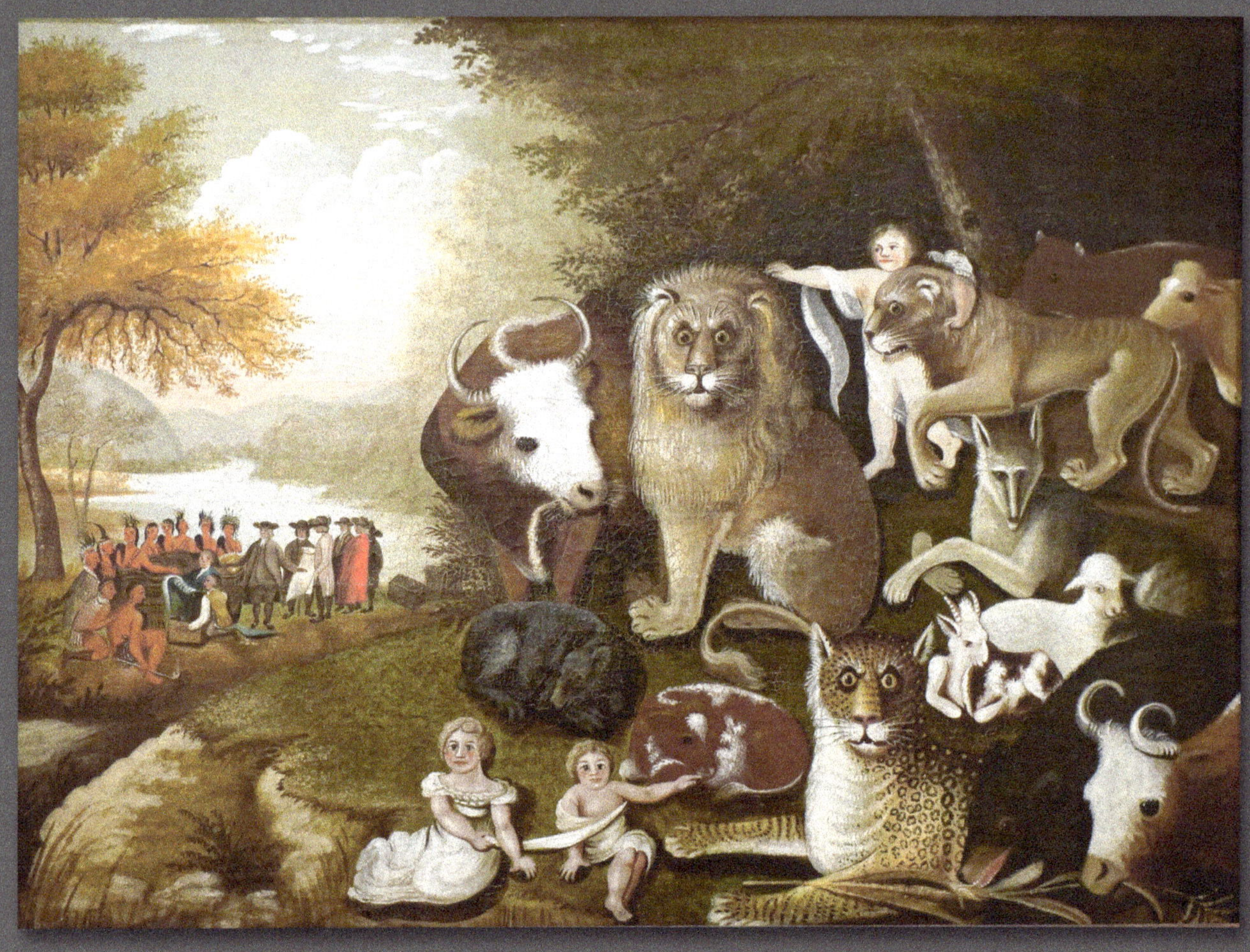

edward hicks
peaceable kingdom (ca. 1833-1834)

Brooklyn Museum
Brooklyn, New York

Ari Mokdad

When the Wolf Dwells with the Lamb

In this modern day *Peaceable Kingdom*,
we could take a selfie on the border of Lebanon and Israel—not
worry about which one of us would return home.

We could walk with animals if
border walls, highways, and parking lots
didn't divide our ~~lands,~~ ~~country,~~ minds.

Our water's polluted, bottled, and sold—
it's been 1,491 days without clean water in Flint,
and we don't know when Line 5 will break.

But this Peaceable Kingdom is digitally connected,
digitally distracted from another bombing,
more diaspora: Gaza, Aleppo, Donbas, Chechnya, Rohingya…

When will it be possible, that the daughter of a Lebanese immigrant
could be accepted in the *Peaceable Kingdom*?
Can all lives finally matter?

This fata morgana on the horizon of Lake Michigan,
opulent silver waves of moonlight;
the mirage of seeing yourself.

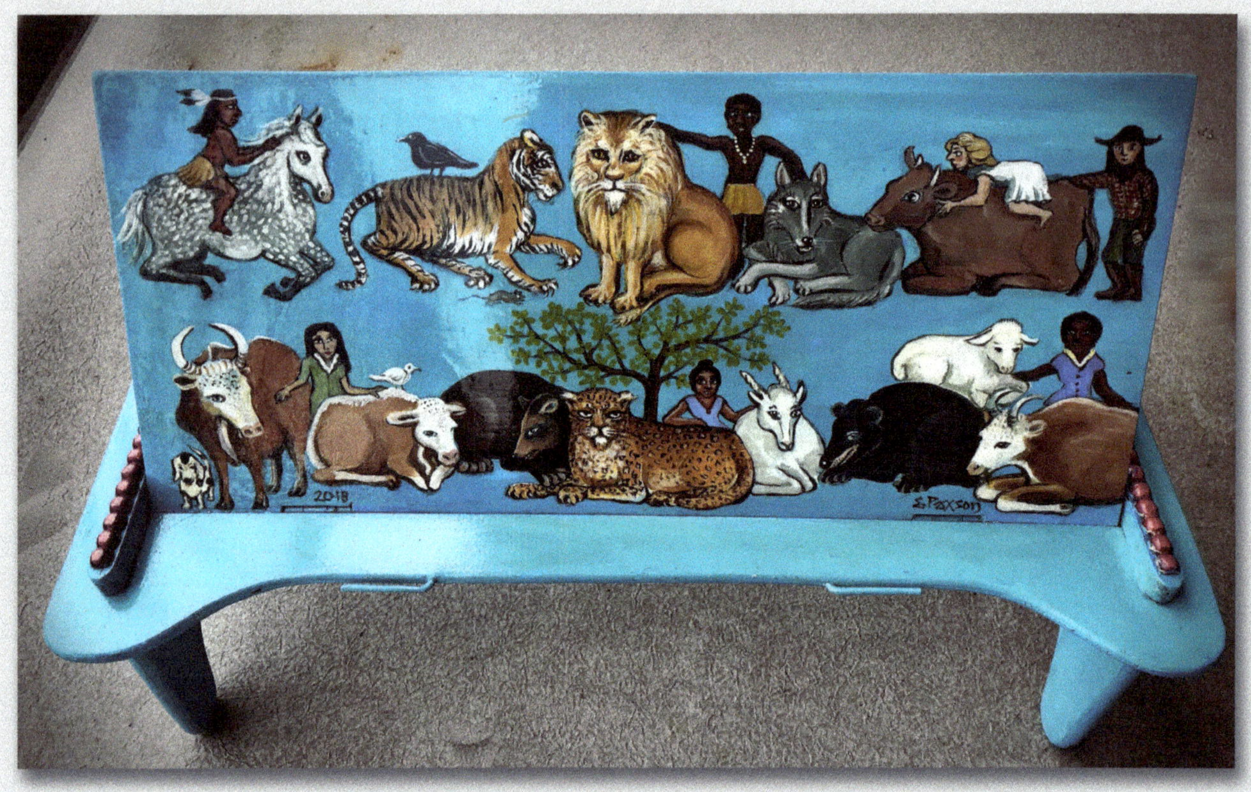

elizabeth paxson

peaceable kingdom lap desk

mixed media
7.5' X 24" X 12"

Because of my Quaker ancestry, Edward Hicks' *Peaceable Kingdom* has always been a favorite of mine. Combining the realism of 19th century art with a charming naive style, Hicks made some 60 versions of his *Peaceable Kingdom*. His folksy depictions of the animals especially lend an innocent vigor. The vintage lap desk, chair and table incorporate animals and people of different races, updating the content somewhat to reflect the ideal of a peaceable kingdom for today..

Greta Bolger

Lap Desk Haibun

ARTWORK: *Peaceable Kingdom Lap Desk* by Elizabeth Paxson

Always sick as a child. Couldn't breathe. Weeks and weeks in bed. Mother sick of me being sick. I could tell by the rough way she pulled up the covers, how she strained to cover the bitter in her voice. *You must be feeling better by now!* But I still hurt all over, no one knew what was wrong. Except Aunt Evelyn, who came by one day with the very best gift I have ever received, a lap desk painted with all kinds of people and animals, living happily together in a perfect blue world. She sat on my bed, hand on my knee, and we named each one. As often as I studied them, I could never see any trace of anger or sadness in their faces. Even the tree was peaceful. From then on, I had two dozen companions who gave me a lovely place to eat, to draw, to solve story problems. When I got better later that year, I moved in with Aunt Evelyn, took my lap desk with me and have kept it close at hand ever since.

Affectionate touch
heals unseen wounds, smooths the path
each one must travel.

Jake Sands

The Council of Might

ARTWORK: *Graffiti Jungle* by Edith Pair

the lamb lies down
with the wolf
but it's the lamb who lies
we already know the wolf's intention
a wolf in his own clothes is
clothed by his own soft diffidence
it's the lamb who makes him a wolf

the child plays with vipers and asps and cobras
in damp dens and nests
but it's the child who's ripe
with reverent venom
faith is blind and choked
with its own ruddy sash
that someone gave the child
and told them not to touch it

cobras don't blink
cobras don't row boats or bear fruit
while women lay with great wings of large eagles

man o man
a mob of meaningless modes
trapped on the river banks
pastures trapped on parapets
the lamb, again, with the ultimate lie

babylon betrays
all rivers dry up seven times over
and men with odd black hats
are the ones who put the fire
in the dead river
anyways

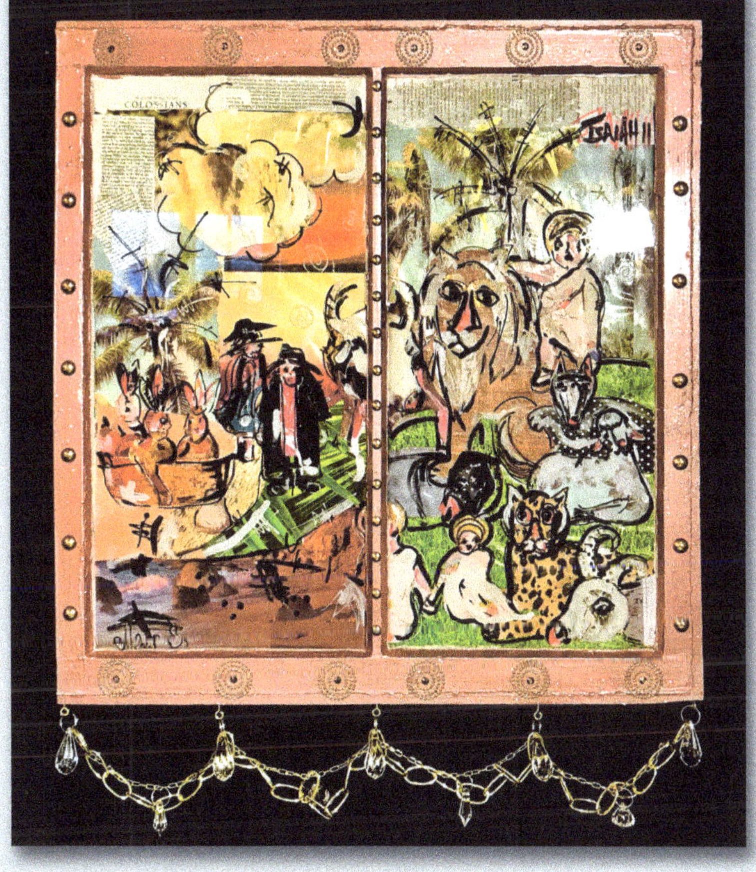

edith pair

graffiti jungle

mixed media on window panel
27" x 27"

My version of *Peaceable Kingdom* by Edward Hicks is aptly titled *Graffiti Jungle* with a modern twist on his original painting. Hicks lived as a Quaker and tried to demonstrate peace amongst animals, man and religion by the transformation from one to another. I took a portion of the Bible from Isaiah and incorporated it into the piece to physically show the original inspiration. I then flattened, distorted and simplified the forms in a graffiti/outsider art style composition to update it to the current era and times we live. This enhances the lyrical flow of ornamental forms and iridescent colors. The primitive savagery of the characters done in paper collage, are in direct opposition with the gentle color on the window frame as the viewer looks out onto the updated "Peaceable Kingdom" we now live. It begs the question—has a peaceful existence gotten better or worse since his original painting was finished … or have the appearance of characters in the painting just changed? Time, technology and modernized living does not prove us to be any closer than the Quakers to finding peace among man, beast and God and if a true Peaceable Kingdom ever does exist—would that be the end as the ultimate goal has finally been achieved?

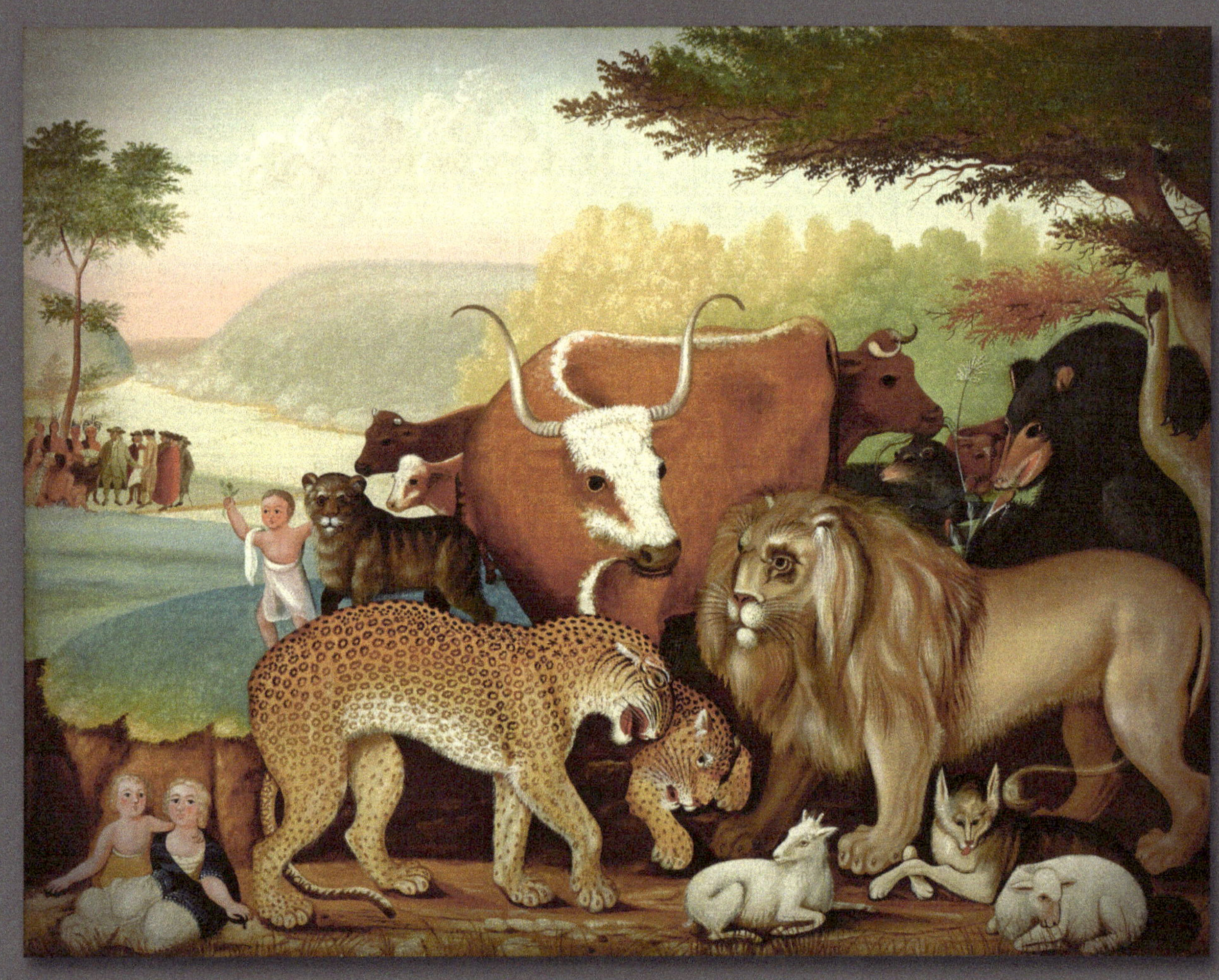

edward hicks
peaceable kingdom (ca. 1846-1847)

Dallas Museum of Art
Dallas, Texas

BC Iler

That Odd Painting from Earth

Zib: *Peaceable Kingdom*—that is the name of the painting.

Xod: Have you seen it?

Zib: Yes. Several versions of it I have seen actually.

Xod: What do you mean?

Zib: The artist did more than one, and others have done artwork inspired by the theme.

Xod: I see… and what exactly is this theme that has been so inspirational?

Zib: Well, that is hard to say.

Xod: Why? Why is it hard to say?

Zib: I am unsure why, but I do know that many things that are hard to say, end up being painted instead of said.

Xod: I do not understand.

Zib: Paintings, and other art forms; they can say things more explicitly and with much more emotion than mere words can.

Xod: Oh? And such is the case with these *Peaceable Kingdom* things?

Zib: Yes. Yes, they say much… very much.

Xod: So then, tell me what they say.

Zib: I will try to try, but, can you not venture down there yourself, to get the message straight from the buxux's mouth? I would gladly go with you.

Xod: No. No I cannot. I am highly allergic to radiation.

Zib: Oh, I am sorry. It is a shame you can't go. There is so much to behold below.

Xod: I know, that is why I stopped here you needling ninny.

Zib: Of course. I apologize, my dear highness… please forgive me.

Xod: Fine, fine. Whateverness. So… the message. What's the message of these 'works' of art?

Zib: Well, again, that's hard to…

Xod: ***Say*** it.

Zib: Okay. It's that all beings should love each other and co-exist peacefully.

Xod: And?

Zib: And that's it.

Xod: Oh? That's it? ***All*** beings? Even Voodaroks & Fluzzerians?

Zib: Yes. Although we, or they, are not specifically depicted in the works.

Xod: Of course not! Because we hate each other and could only co-exist peacefully after one of us had completely obliterated the other into utter extinction.

Zib: That is sad.

Xod: That is reality. Perhaps I shall commission a painting of a Voodarok lasering to death a hundred Fluzzerians all at once, and call it… 'War-able Kingdom.'

Zib: That is sadder yet.

Xod: Why? Did these ridiculous *Peaceable Kingdom* paintings bring peace to the human people of Earth?

Zib: Perhaps so… a little maybe.

Xod: Well that is a little hard to tell now, isn't it? Amongst the endless bomb craters and the glowing green fog that encircles this bilious biohazard.

Zib: Maybe if more people had gotten the message… if more had seen the painting they…

Xod: ***Enough*** about that devilish doodle! I've made up my minds. We are not taking one thing from this pitiful planet. Nope. Not one painting, not one sculpture, and not one book—***nothing***. There is no message of importance here to share with our people. The Earthlings 'art' work is like a contagious disease that is capable of sickening entire societies and causing mass destruction. Obviously.

Zib: Okay, but…

Xod: No buts.

Zib: Oh please, your majesty, I beg you, just one but.

Xod: Well… okay Zib. One but, but only one but.

Zib: Thank you. But the music. May we please take their music.

Xod: Hmm… the music? I haven't heard any of their music. What's it like? Is it as demented and dangerous as the rest of their doings?

Zib: No. No, not at all. It is wonderful, and it was created merely for enjoyment and dancing, without messages or themes, or trying to say anything serious, and they ***never*** wrote songs criticizing their governments, or complaining about social injustices.

Xod: Really!?

Zib: Yes, and actually, they had a golden rule about ***not ever*** singing songs meant to protest war, or attempting to influence anyone to question authority, and they certainly had ***no*** songs about peace.

Xod: Good! Well that is refreshing to hear. Our people could sure use more mindless entertainment, and we really shouldn't go home empty handed… okay, okay, we can take the music.

Zib: Thank you very, very much. I'll go get it immediately. I think our people will appreciate this music highly. Especially the albums from the late 1960s.

Xod: Oh? Is that when it was at its most mindless?

Zib: Uh, yes. Yes, absolutely indeed.

Xod: Good, good. Now hurry up. This place is starting to give me the creeps.

Zib: Right away my grace!

FIN

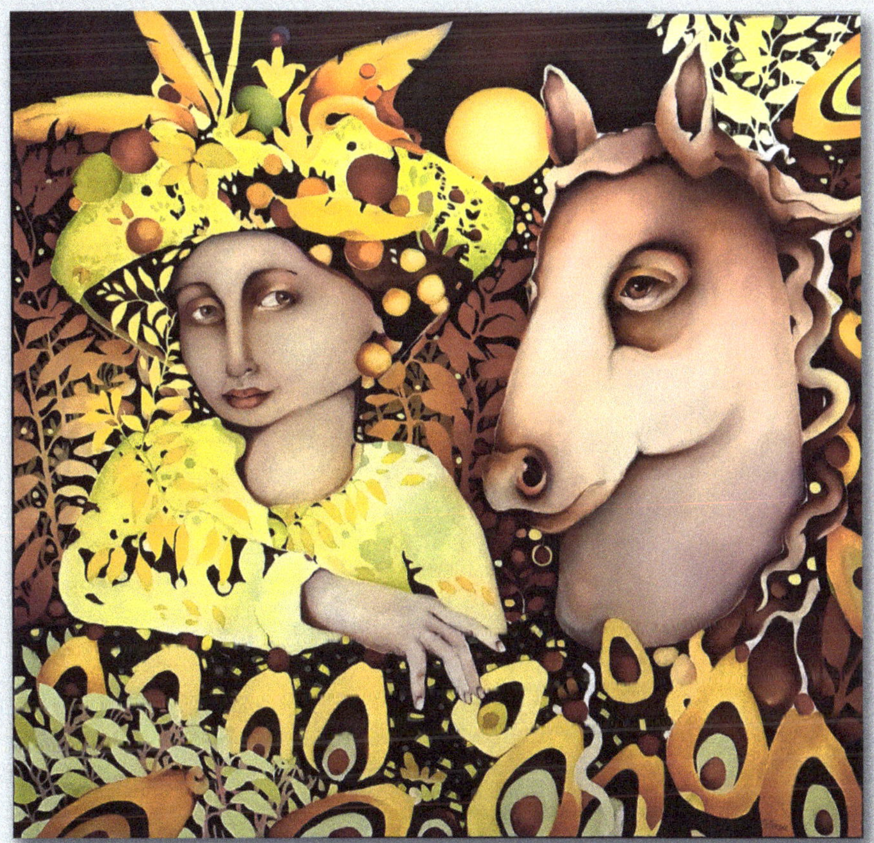

jim matherne
cricket song

oil
42″ x 44″

I was inspired by the work of Edward Hicks, primarily because of the peaceful interaction between people and animals. Many of his works show people holding, touching, and embracing animals. This is in stark contrast with many other artists of the time that depicted animals being hunted, killed, or shown as trophies. Hunting plaques with images of dead animals strapped together were common in paintings and in furniture (i.e., Black Forest). When I was growing up, a large part of my life centered around my passion for animals. Ponds, creeks, lakes, and the woods were where I spent most of my time. The love of animals and the outdoors has influenced my art work for the past 40 years. The inspirations and influences: artist Edward Hicks, my friend Ward's horse, artist Gustav Klimt, the hat in a photo of Thomas Edison and his wife, Mina. The painting *Cricket Song* tries to capture that peaceful time.

Susan Odgers

Dialogos

In Traverse City, I went to both the Michigan Artists Gallery and Higher Art Gallery to explore the exhibit inspired by the Edward Hicks' painting *Peaceable Kingdom*. At the Michigan Artists Gallery, an invisible force seemed to pull me towards Mitchell Truemner's painting *Peaceable Moves* and away from the other works in the riverside gallery. The painting depicts a bear and bull playing chess under a tree on a summery day.

Tracy Chevalier, an American-British historical novelist has studied selective responses to works of art. Her YouTube TEDSalon London 2012 presentation, "Finding the Story Inside the Painting" has been viewed over 1.3 million times. While touring a museum or gallery, Chevalier advises us to return to a work of art that slows us down. As we look deeply, what do we see? The story we see in a painting, fills in the gap between what we know about the artist and subject and what we don't know. There's creative power for the viewer in the lack of resolution. Chevalier wrote a novel about the *Girl with the Pearl Earring*, which was later adapted into the 2003 film starring Colin Firth and Scarlett Johansson.

Merriam-Webster defines *ekphrasis* as a literary description of or commentary on a visual work of art. I would add that the beauty and freedom of ekphrastic writing is that each of us can project our interior life onto the work of art. The written pieces, even in response to the same works of art, are as different as the individual writers. Likewise, Truemner's portrayal of Hicks "Peaceable Kingdom" seems another form of *ekrphasis*. Over 70 visual artists participated in the exhibit. No two pieces are alike.

After gazing at Truemner's painting for a long time, I read his artist statement displayed next to the painting:

> We all live near a proverbial cliff, some of us are well are of that, some of us are much more oblivious. Be careful, it can be a long way down. We are ALL trying to avoid the cliffs while playing the game. Some of us participate, while

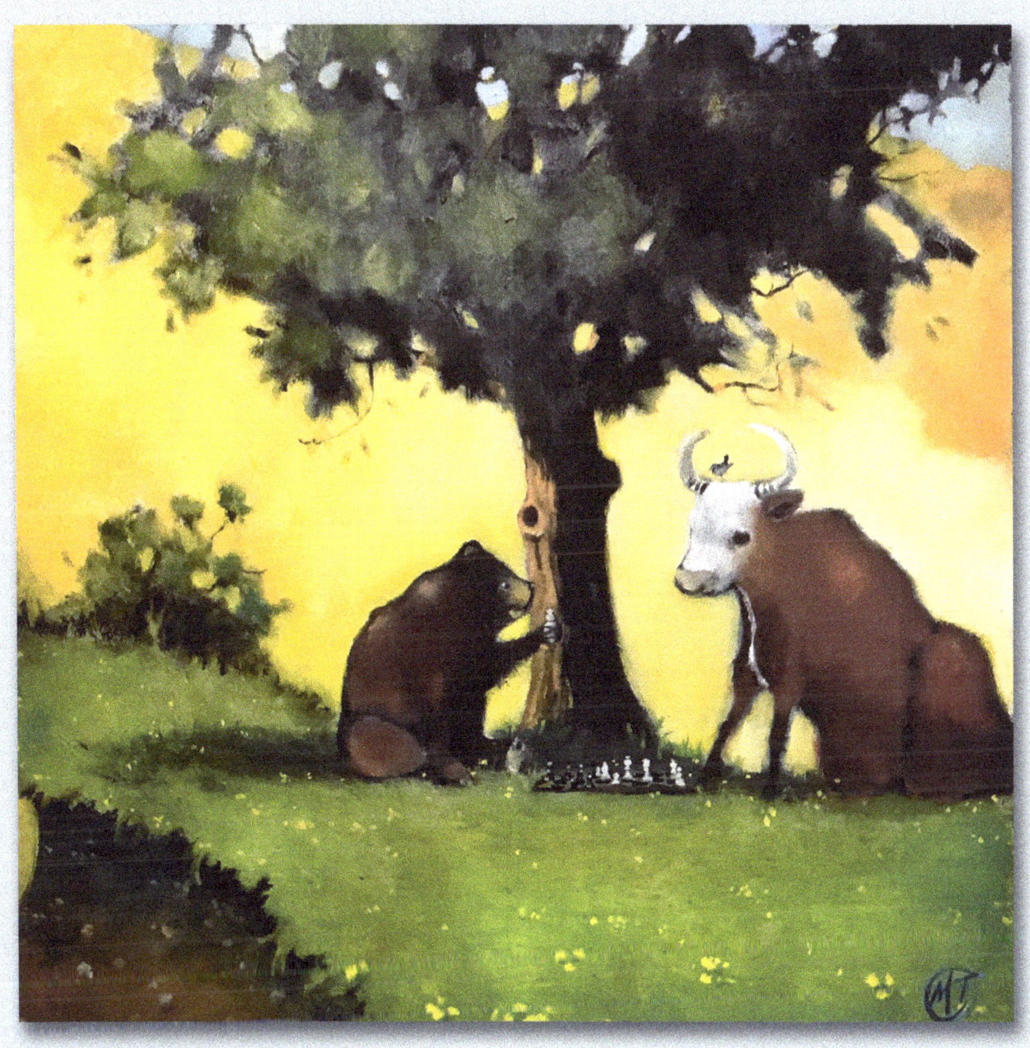

mitch truemner

peaceable moves

oil on canvas

20″ X 20″

> others would rather be bystanders, watching all of the action. The participants need to be careful, the bystanders need not complain of the outcome... Every move has consequences. Choose your next move wisely ... while you are making your moves, realize that we are all different from one another. But our commonality is that we are all doing our best to win and not fall off the edge.

Leaving the gallery, I wanted to know more about how Truemner saw his work. I went to a nearby coffee shop and emailed him. To my delight, he answered my questions almost immediately; even when I wrote to him a second time. By directly engaging with the artist, I deepened my relationship with him, the painting and my writing task.

Email Correspondence

SUSAN: WHAT DO YOU THINK ARE THE EDGES, CLIFFS? IS A BYSTANDER just playing a different game? What's winning?

MITCHELL: The "cliffs" are the pitfalls, the bad decisions we make in life, some are small and have no lasting effect on us or the people around us, others are larger, more destructive to ourselves and tend to ripple outward to more lives than we know, leaving scars that last a lifetime. We all have "cliffs" nearby ... in one way or another. Some of us are well aware of how close we are to those cliffs, others are not aware, living on the edge every day.

SUSAN: The bystanders?

MITCHELL: The bystanders are ones that may have many opinions on how "The Game" is played but tends to never jump into the games themselves ... waiting for others to make the decisions that affect their lives, and then leaving it all up to fate. They tend to be the ones that complain the loudest about the outcome of the game. They tend to be the very ones that are self-proclaimed experts on the game ... but would never consider actually playing, "all in" to make the moves necessary to win the game.

SUSAN: Tell me more about the game.

MITCHELL: The Game—this is really very simple. Life. The playing of the game, and how we play is sometimes ... often times, more important than winning the game. In a sense ... in my opinion, life, (the game) is more gratifying, richer ... by playing the right moves that help others, bring joy to others, make life easier for others ... in a way, make their game playing moves easier. Winning? Well, funny thing ... I have discovered that by helping others win their "Game" I also win as well.

We all come from different upbringing, different education, different time and place ... it all helps form who we are ... no wonder, we think differently about the game and how it should be played. But, when it really comes down to it, we are all just trying to win our own game and hopefully, in the process, we give ourselves some credit, that we made some pretty, darn good moves.

SUSAN: As a practical point, I don't know a lot about chess. Is the bear holding the king? Tell me about the pieces on the board ... is someone winning?

MITCHELL: No, the chess piece is just any old chess piece ... there was no thought into who was winning. With the right moves from each player, everyone wins.

DAYS LATER, I RETURNED TO THE GALLERY WITH A YOUNG FRIEND, A recent university graduate. "Let's play," I said. "What do you see in Truemner's painting?"

My friend described the content. Then, hesitating, she said "I don't know what I'm supposed to see. What do *you* see, Susan?"

"There isn't anything you're *supposed* to see," I said. "I think most of us are often intimidated by art. We think we have to like and be educated about all of it. I'll share what my first impressions were when I looked at this painting. Before I wrote the artist or did any other research. Those first thoughts and feelings made me want to stay with this painting and enter into it over and over again."

Inside a Writer's Notebook

ONE A BRIGHT SUMMERY DAY, I SEE A BEAR AND A BULL PLAYING CHESS under the shade of an oak tree at the foot of the Sleeping Bear Dunes National Lakeshore on Lake Michigan, five miles north of Empire. The sand dunes form a 260 foot wall behind the tree. The yellow flowers throughout the green grass don't tell me if it's spring and they're dandelions or summers' blooming Coreopis wildflowers. To the side of the bear there's a ravine or rip in the earth that looks like the bear and bull are on raised ground … a sort of island. A songbird sits atop the bull's head between its horns. The bear is brown and sits on its bottom, legs out in front. The bull has a brown body and white face. The bull is balancing on its two vertically extended front legs, in a sitting, leaning forward position. There's a softness to the bear and bull's facial expressions. They're having a conversation. The painting has both an allegory and animation feel to it.

The bear is holding the bull's King; winning the chess game. The chess pieces are black and white; the bear plays the black pieces. I can hear Patty Smith's song "Peaceable Kingdom" about broken love playing in the background: "Maybe one day we'll be strong enough To build it back again, Build the peaceable kingdom Back again, Build it back again."

I'm thinking about Hicks' Quaker values of equality, peace, community and stewardship of the earth. What's the meaning of life, our nature and purpose? Is there more than animalistic survival?

The bear and bull represent the positions in the US financial market!!!! The chess game is the economy or the source of all of the world's resources. And, resource allocation is the source of war, peace.

But in Truemner's painting, the bull and the bear are not as we humans have manipulated them as symbols of positive or negative. Bear and bull respect the need for the other; the balance to keep the world in check, safe, normal. They aren't rivals. In nature, there are ups and downs. Yin and yang.

Their conversation is like that of other famous pairs; Christopher Robin and Winnie the Pooh, Batman and the Joker and Andre Gregory and Wallace Shawn in Louis Malle's film, *My Dinner With Andre.*

The bear lives in the wild, forages for food, is homeless, an explorer, tries new foods, thrives on what is fresh. The bull is domesticated, contained, farm fed, imprisoned, lives as livestock as an economic value … is cared for … and can help the bear survive the lean months.

The bull fights opponents with its horns tilted up in the air; symbolizing strong results, trading to once-unthinkable highs … bonds/currencies/ commodities … all growth is good … the market now has a sci-fi feel to it. The bear fights opponents by pawing downward … signifying falling market prices, pessimism, that it's OK for the economy to not always be growing. Not a crash but a retreat. The bear is more powerful than the bull. This is not Teddy Roosevelt's teddy bear.

Cliff, precipice, broken land, divided. Corporations make money, no matter what.

Which moment in history would I use as my the backdrop in the painting? Hicks painted nearly 100 versions of the *Peaceable Kingdom.* Maybe I'd use the Black men harassed in Starbucks or the *Fearless Girl* by Kristen Visbal—a bronze statue on Wall Street … across from the *Charging Bull* by Arturo Di Modica.

Yes, it's all there in the painting. I see, hear, smell, taste and can feel it. And, you?

■

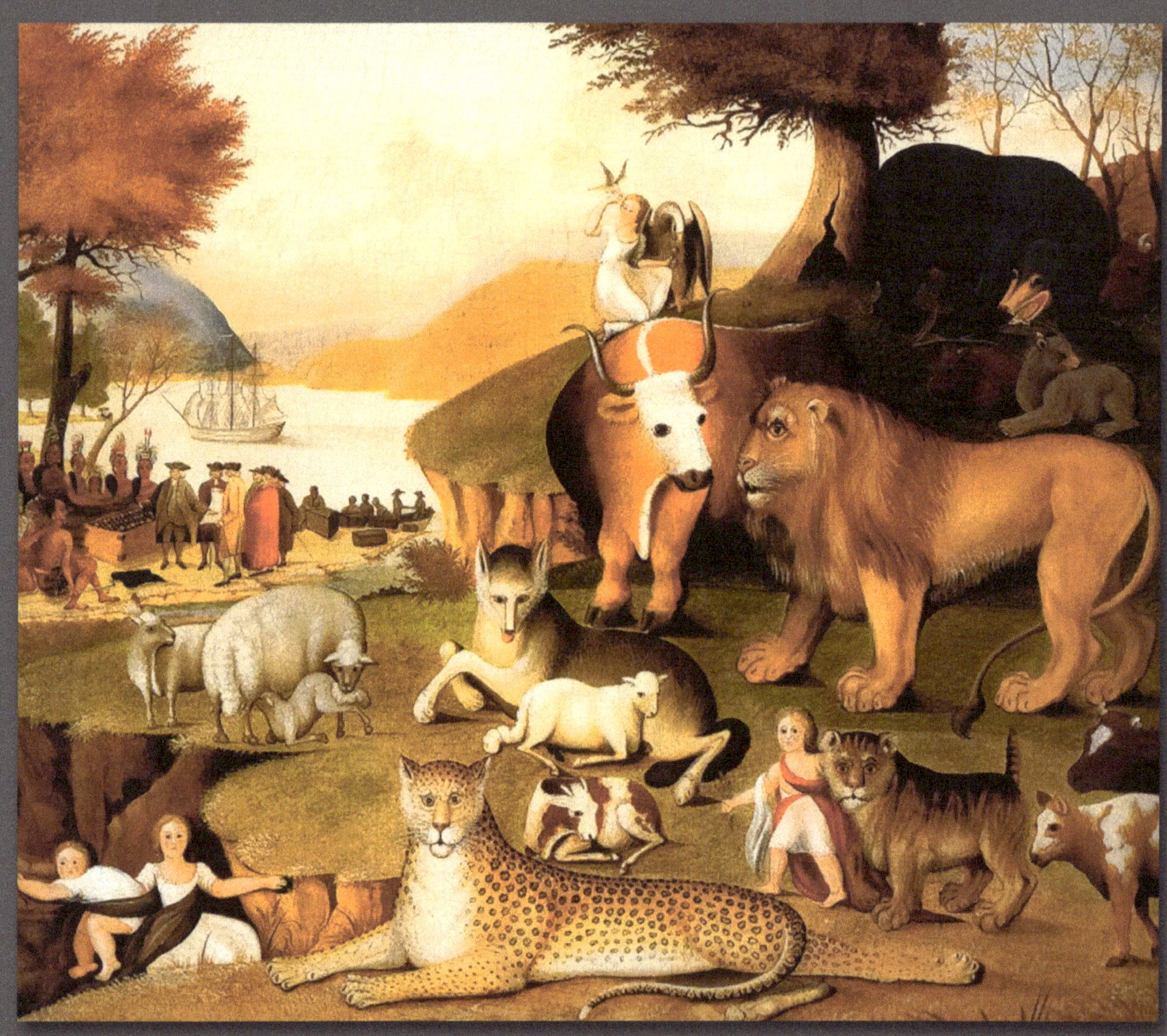

edward hicks
peaceable kingdom (ca. 1846-1848)

Private Collection

Bob McQuilkin

Peaceable Kingdom

It is a once upon a time of humanity
growing out of a weariness with tribal
outrage and endless cat fits,
snarling tempers and clawing animosity.

We dream a dream of a day to come
when we will be tranquillized
of differences and freed from fear
of not having enough territory to feed.

We dream the scene of unlikely
possibilities keeping alive our hope
that within our spirit there is desire
to give in to embracing a divine truce.

JoAnna Pepe

La Donna Guarda Negli Occhi Del Leone: The Woman Gazes Into The Eyes Of The Lion

It was the afternoon of April 30, 1998, when I sought refuge in Chiesa di San Michele in the walled city of Lucca. Rain pummeled the streets while I sat in a stone pew and stared at a lion etched in a marble column.

Insulated from the blaring horns of cab drivers shouting *Cane Dio, Dio Cane,* Dog God, God Dog, at Vespa drivers weaving in and out of traffic, I shivered in damp wool, wondered about the lion and if it mollified the pagans who feigned conversion to the pope's religion, like it did my nonna.

When she was twelve Nonna Guiseppina crocheted a lace table cloth that was the envy of all the old women, *tutte le vecchie* in the small town of Bom Pietro where she grew up. Centered in the lace was a lion. *Why a lion?* I have asked that question for years but never of my nonna. And now this morning *il leone* wants to speak and I, *la donna* want to listen.

"Your nonna needed *coraggio*—a strong heart to bear the loss of her mother who died of female problems shortly after the table cloth was completed. Superstition forbade her to utter the words "uterine cancer," and risk more illness upon *la famiglia*—the four siblings your nonna raised after her mother died.

For thirteen years nonna cooked, cleaned, tended the garden, wove linens and sewed for *la famiglia*. Infused with *il coraggio* she lived by the rule of her father's Sicilian law until the day she boarded the ship to Ellis Island with a packed trousseau containing a lion in lace surrounded by vines of roses, circles, diamonds and stars. And now 90 years later—the lace, fecund and pristine wants you to hold court with the lion from Bom Pietro."

■

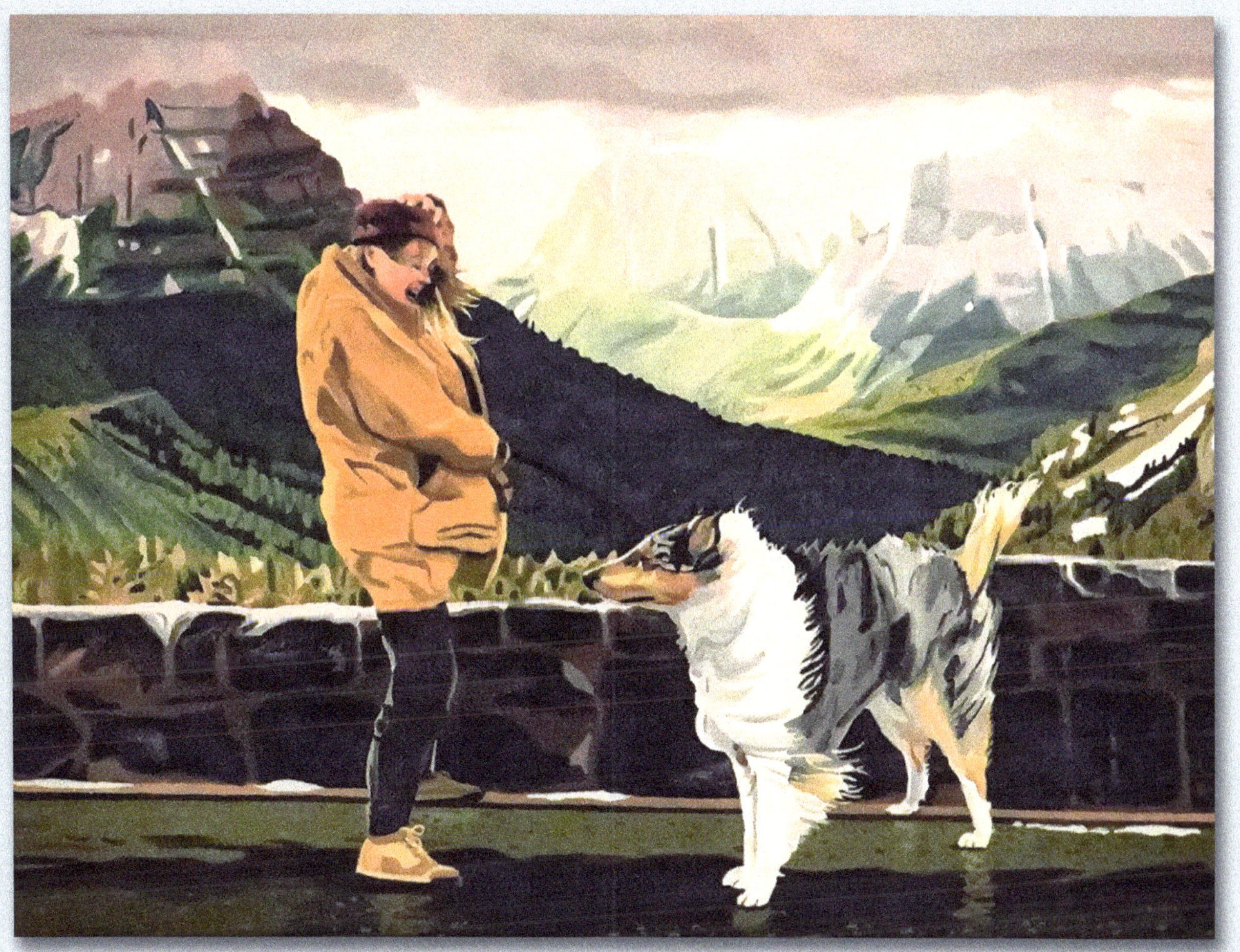

steve toornman

continental divide

oil

20.5" x 20"

For me the idea of a "Peaceable Kingdom" occurs when we have personal relationships with other than the human species. Animals take us out of ourselves because they live in the moment and they are not inclined to worry too much about anything. During the experiences we have together there is no time for us to dwell on our personal problems, we are also living in the moment. This creates the *Peaceable Kingdom*.

Paul Maxbauer

Desire For The Peaceable Kingdom

Oh, to achieve the Peaceable Kingdom, long our hearts' desire. Peacefulness,
a stillness of heart, mind and body, long the artist's goal.

Animals living free from the rule of instinct, the wolf and lamb,
calf and young lion, friends forevermore.

The cow and bear, leopard and kid, the child and adder, friends too!
Who can accomplish a world so transformed, a return to the Garden?

No human effort alone will suffice. From Afghanistan to Syria, Gaza to
Yemen, indeed to the ends of the earth, the ground is stained with blood.

Yet, as the prophet reminds us, the promise remains: "None shall hurt
or destroy on all my holy mountain."

Who can bring about the Peaceable Kingdom? Isaiah points to the shoot
from the lineage of David. Will our hearts be open to recognize and receive Him?

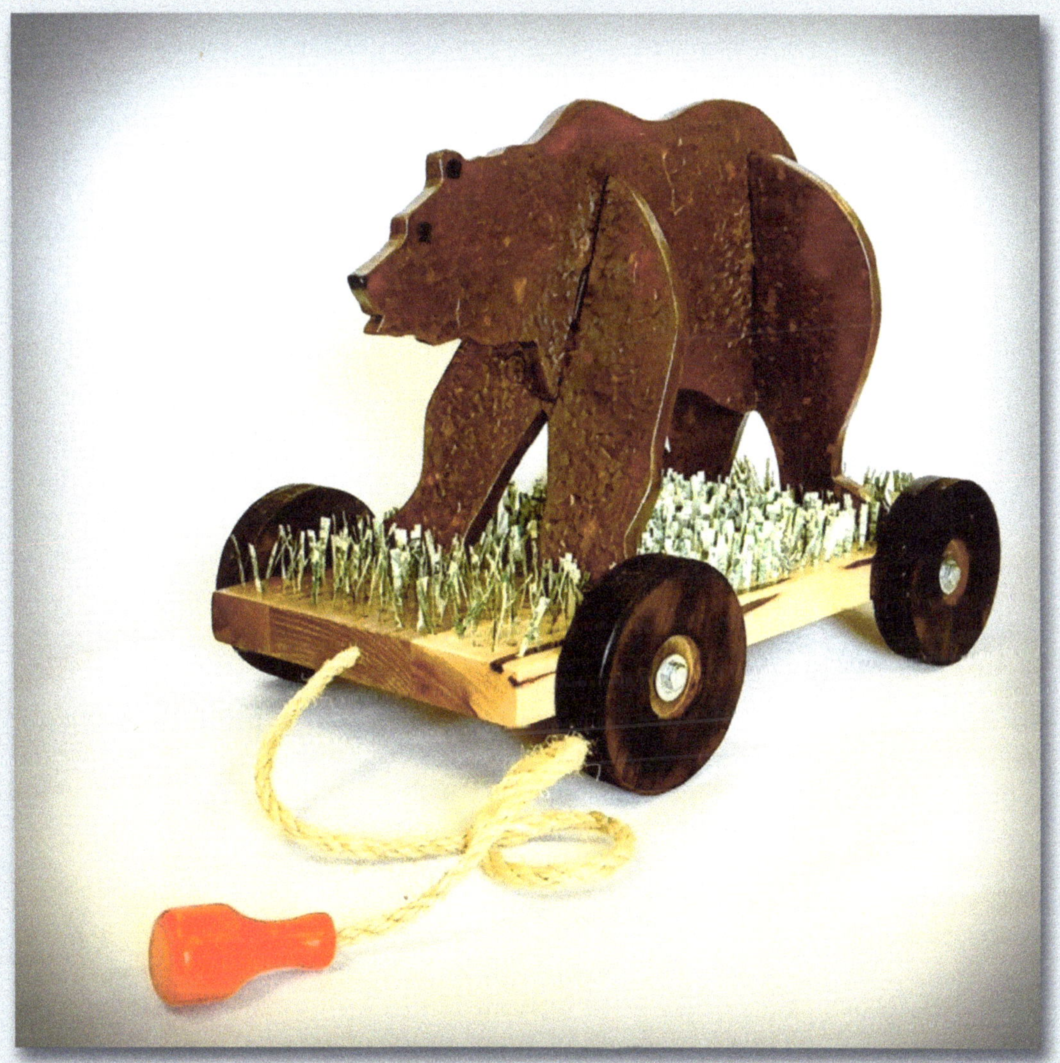

corey and stacey bechler
american bear

clay, wood and money
14" x 17" x 11"

This is a funky mixed media sculpture, inspired by the bear in the painting by Edward Hicks.This mixed media sculpture is a combination of clay, wood, and genuine United States Money. This bear pull toy is a reflection and combination of the Americana of yesteryears with the fun and whimsy of today!

Luise Bolleber

Walls

The sheer joy of the people who were nimble enough to clamber atop the wall in Berlin that night in 1989 was infectious. They crowded themselves on the thin lip of the wall like gulls on a pier, some of them pounding vigorously at the hated concrete with hammers and chisels, participating in the beginning of its destruction and tossing graffiti-sprayed chunks of history to the crowds below. Only the day before, they would have been shot for being up there. The revelers were in full celebration mode after the East German government announced that all German Democratic Republic citizens could freely visit West Germany and West Berlin.

I happened to be in another divided country, Cyprus, when I watched the historic celebration taking place. It was a pivotal moment for me, the kind you never forget, like how everyone remembers where they were and what they were doing when they found out about the space shuttle explosion or 9/11 disaster. I was sitting with my Greek Cypriot boyfriend on our couch in our apartment, and the jubilation playing out on the TV screen rose up in me like a tidal wave. I was thrilled that my parents' homeland was on its way to reunification. I was travel savvy by the time I was a teenager, having flown with my mother across the Atlantic many times to visit our relatives in West Germany. But I had never visited East Germany. How odd and wonderful it was, for the next few years to simply say or write, "Germany." I was so used to writing West Germany when I scribbled my relatives' addresses on airmail envelopes. After 40 years of a fissured nation, blissful, inclusive peace settled over the German republic. East Germans could go anywhere they wanted, whenever they wanted. They were free. It must have been as wonderful as tasting ice cream for the first time; sweet, highly satisfying, and addictive. But the same could not be said for my boyfriend Sotiris. He was not free to go where he wanted in his country.

§ § §

CYPRUS REMINDED ME OF SOUTHERN CALIFORNIA WHERE I HAD RECENTLY lived. Sunshine abounded and the midnight blue Mediterranean Sea offered fantastic beaches and plentiful fresh seafood. Our apartment was in Paphos on the southwest coast of this small island where Greek is the dominant language. On weekends we explored his country. He showed me the rocky outcropping on the seashore that's known as the birthplace of Aphrodite. We visited the Tombs of the Kings necropolis and the pine forested Troodos Mountains where we stayed in an elegant lodge and watched swallows flit back and forth between the forest and the overhanging eave by our window, where their nests hung like globular mud fruit. He taught me how to drive his manual transmission Volkswagen Golf. As happy as we were, though, Sotiris' soul found no permanent peace. And, he declared, he never would until the divided parts of his country were reunited. A mere 75 miles away from us, a barb-wired demarcation known as the Green Line snaked across the craggy landscape, ripping this idyllic island into separate north and south entities. And just like it had been for the East Germans for 40 years, Sotiris was not free to cross that line.

Like many countries, Cyprus has a long history of occupation and control by other nations. But in 1974, Cyprus history took a dark turn and changed Sotiris' life forever. Greek Cypriot Nationalists staged a coup d'etat in an attempt to incorporate Cyprus into Greece. This action prompted an invasion by Turkey, ostensibly to protect Turkish Cypriots. The invasion led to the seizure of what is today's Turkish Republic of Cyprus, a state that is recognized only by Turkey and that encompasses nearly one third of the island.

IN THE EARLY MORNING OF JULY 26, 1974, BEFORE THE SUN HAD A CHANCE to tinge the horizon, screams pierced the still air in the small village of Agridaki and woke 14-year-old Sotiris from a deep sleep. People from Sysklipos, the village next door, rushed through the streets in a panic. They had fled their homes in advance of an onslaught of Turkish army tanks and warned everyone to leave immediately. The Turks were headed this way and

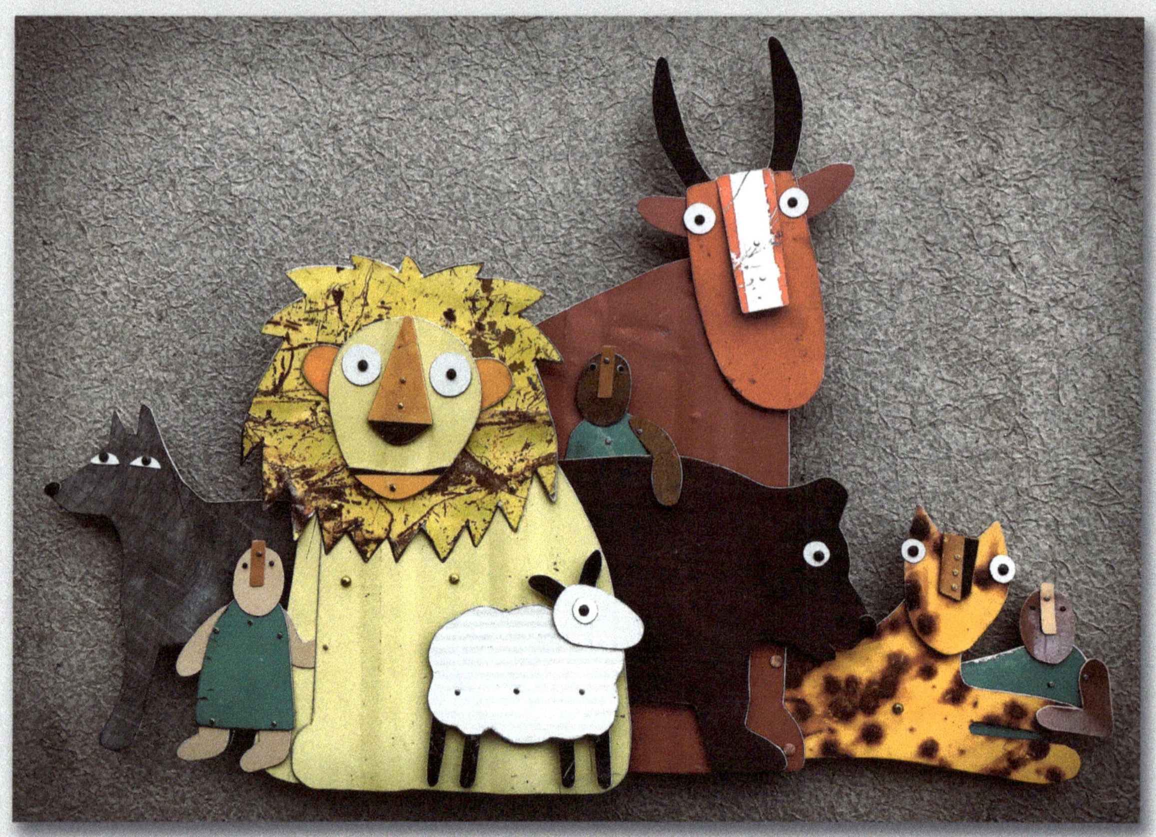

scott randolph

peace & the animals … no politicians

recycled metal/mixed media
14″ x 24″

Edward Hicks, the artist who inspired my piece, painted his version of the of the passage from Isaiah 62 times over the course of his life. The idea that the "wolf shall dwell with lamb, and the leopard shall lie down with the young goat" is a potent metaphor for a peace that is so close if only we allow spirit into our hearts. There are so many cases of children being raised by animals, and I have always taken this a sign of a child's innocence and pure, nonthreatening nature. My piece highlights this connection and possibility. Hicks included a sub narrative of the Quakers meeting with Native Americans in peace and harmony, and while this was a noble vision and wish, it was not to be. I chose to portray a world with just the children and animals, as the words and deeds of men and politics seem to constantly get in the way of fulfilling this prophecy. Peace in the heart of a child and an animal is sometime I can believe in.

an attack was imminent. As the news spread, forming a wake of alarmed families spilling out of their houses from one end of the village to the the other, Sotiris heard explosions in the distance and smelled smoke drifting up from the burning forest. There was no time to grab valuables, food, or even clothing. Chaos ensued as everyone tried to find an immediate means of escape. Cars and buses were few in the village but Sotiris' father owned a commercial van into which the whole family and as many neighbors as could fit, ranging in age from 2 to 80, packed themselves, barely able to breathe. They drove south to the capital, Nicosia, joining an exodus of thousands of others.

Sotiris' elderly grandparents in the next village managed to escape on foot through the forest a day later. His aunt, who was blind, did not make it out. Stories of atrocities filtered in of murders, rapes and looting. The events of Sotiris' family played out all across the Northern region of the island, displacing over 150,000 people. They had fled with only the clothes on their backs, becoming refugees in their own country. To this day over 1600 people are still missing.

IT WAS HARD FOR ME TO BELIEVE THAT THIS PERSON WHO WAS NEAR and dear to me had had to run for his life, leaving everything he owned behind, and that he could have perished at the hands of marauding soldiers. When I was 14, I was shopping for jeans and joining throngs of other teens in the halls of my high school in the suburbs of Detroit. What happened to Sotiris and his family seemed like the kind of thing you read about in history books, happening generations, or hundreds of years ago. How could something like this happen in my generation? I tried to imagine the terror, the confusion, and the shock of having to flee in order to save your own life. But I think that unless you personally witness an event as devastating as a foreign invasion, you can't really fathom what it was like or how the experience still moves and breathes within you, forever casting a pall on the days of your life. You can't know what peace is.

In 2003, Turkey and Cyprus reached an agreement and opened the border, allowing passage between the areas. It was a mostly symbolic gesture, however, and not a true reunification; property that had been confiscated was not returned to its rightful Greek Cypriot owners. People were only allowed to make day visits, and Greek Cypriots had to show their passports at the checkpoints, a point that rankled Sotiris so much that for a long time he refused to cross the border, even though other family members ventured across to visit their old home. As hopeful as it seemed that the people of north and south Cyprus could now mingle, there was just too much that hadn't been addressed, the murders of thousands, the mass grave burials, and other monstrosities. And now, a grisly discovery brought the horror back full force. Some of Sotiris' family returned to his aunt's home to investigate her fate. Her body had been buried in a shallow grave in her yard. She had been beheaded.

I BECAME TRULY FOND OF CYPRUS WHEN I LIVED THERE AND TODAY enjoy drinking from the memory of my time there. I loved Sotiris but he and I parted as friends. He could not abandon his torn country to be with me in the U.S. And as much as his family had welcomed me and the beauty of his Mediterranean island home had charmed me, I too felt the pull of my country. America, as Europeans call the U.S., my big, geographically diverse, wild-at-heart country was calling me home.

I hadn't realized just how much I identified with being an American. I had lived in Germany as a preteen and experienced some homesickness then, but living abroad as an adult was different. I could embrace the faraway country I was in while pondering what it means to be a U.S. citizen. And what it means to be a free person. I had no idea that a country at peace with itself, my country, was something to be grateful for.

The situation in Cyprus today remains complicated. Various attempts at reconciliation over the years have failed and peace still seems like a mirage in the desert, shimmering in hopefulness but empty in hand. If only Aphrodite, the Greek goddess of love, could rise up again out of the sea and wield her power to bring the conflicting sides together. It's my hope that the people of Cyprus will find a workable solution in my lifetime, and that Sotiris can find peace. He deserves that. It's what we all deserve.

■

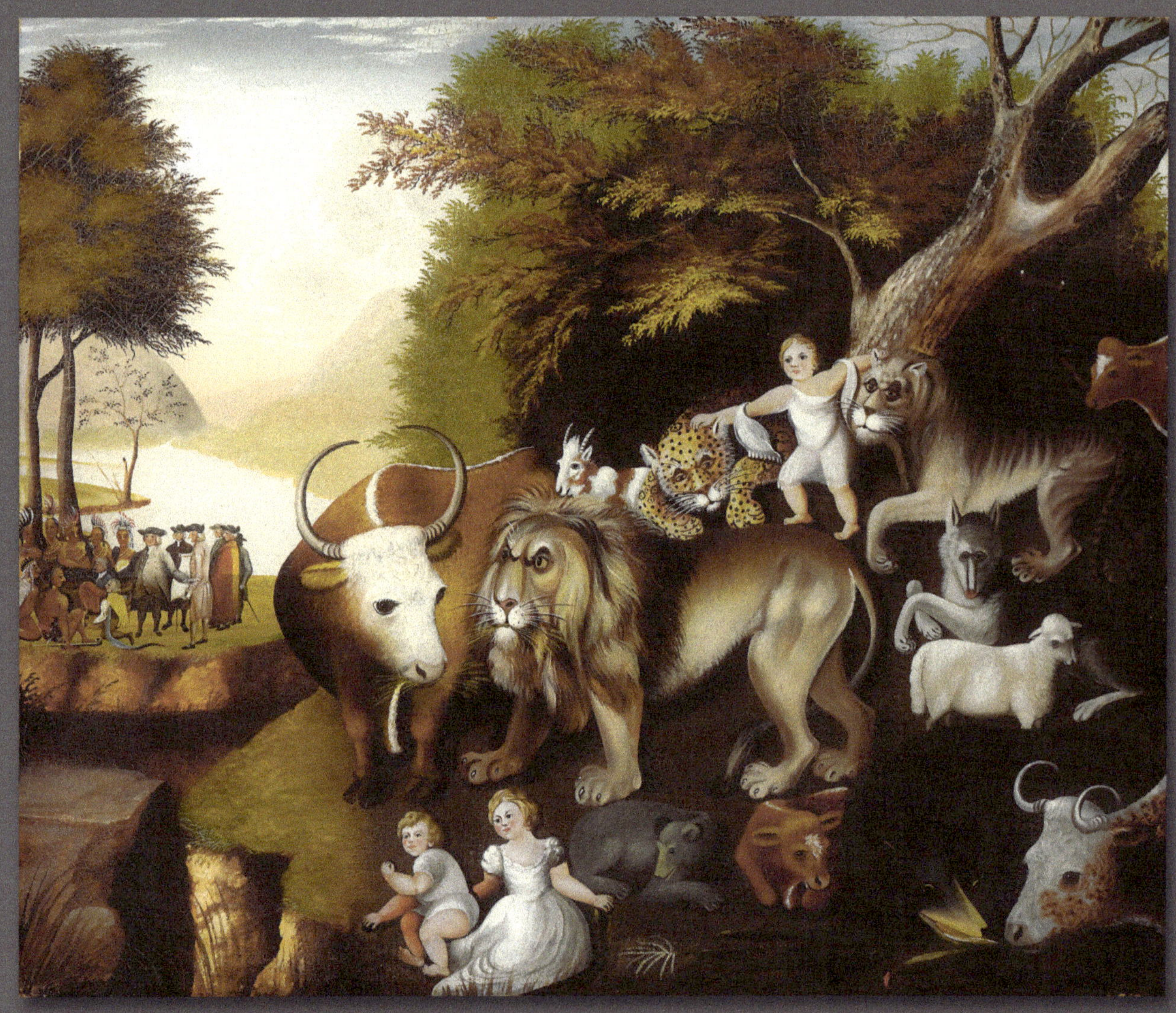

edward hicks
peaceable kingdom (ca. 1849)

Private Collection

Marina Call

CAPISCI?

"Fuckin' READ the instructions. *Capisci?*" the teacher said.

Honestly, this is what I wished I could say. But instead uttered, "You will have 30 minutes to complete the assignment quietly. Don't read the instructions once, or twice, but THREE times before you ask me any questions. *Capisci?*"

Twenty seconds weren't allowed to pass before I saw a hand go up. I didn't even have to look. It was K-lee, that name I hated so much and always got wrong, KAley, KEYley, KIley. Why the fuck would parents choose this name? Choose it and then spell it in hieroglyphics. Experience had taught me— the poorer the school district, the higher the letter count. This girl in particular won the grand prize with 10 letters:

K-a-e-y-l-e-i-g-h-e.

"What is it? I said, looking up from my iPad.

"Do we need to write the assignment in I-talian?" She was thrilled to hear her voice.

My head searched the overcrowded classroom.

"What class are we in?" I dispassionately asked.

"Italian, but I—" she started.

I interrupted her with a raised hand, saving her from her own stupidity.

Whoever said there was no such thing as a stupid question was obviously an idiot, and had never taught some of my third grade students.

The most fascinating thing about teaching was seeing it all, on the other side of the curtain.

The teacher's lounge was a bitchfest of sorts.

"Oh, that Amanda girl, she will be pregnant by her first year of high school. I can bet on it," the math teacher said.

The language arts teacher chimed in, "I wish Greyson's dad wouldn't forget to give him his meds. On Wednesday mornings I can always tell his eyes are crazy and it's gonna be one of those days."

On the other side of the lounge the new teacher explained, "Hannah is a klepto. Last week she took a pen box and the Hello Kitty stickers. Today, I found the neon orange sticky notes in her backpack and she flat out denied it. She is only in second grade!"

Even the librarian was unhappy, "They just took away my prep time to do recess duty. I didn't go to school to watch kids play tag! They don't pay me enough for this crap!"

Ever since I started teaching I realized it was somehow a payback. I had asked too many questions of my teachers. I hoped none had been as dumb as Kaeyleighe's.

The classroom was quiet, mostly, and my hand was shaking on the paper- containing my anger. No, it wasn't anger, more like disbelief. Did I roll my eyes at the children? I did not remember my teachers doing that to me. I wondered if that was legal?

My own fifth grade teacher had once said, "I don't have favorites. You are all my favorites when you do your best." That tone: *do your best, do your best.*

I wasn't doing my best. Within fifteen seconds of meeting a child I knew which ones were my favorites.

Third grade was the last stop on the train. The innocence barometer was high since they still believed in Santa Claus and didn't use the dirty words their "one friend" had told them and their bodies stayed with them, within them, not protruding and rounding out. They were contained and their smells did not smell.

That day, the last day I saw them finish third grade, I cried a little, knowing the summer would wash their belief in magic and push them closer to our world, the adult world.

■

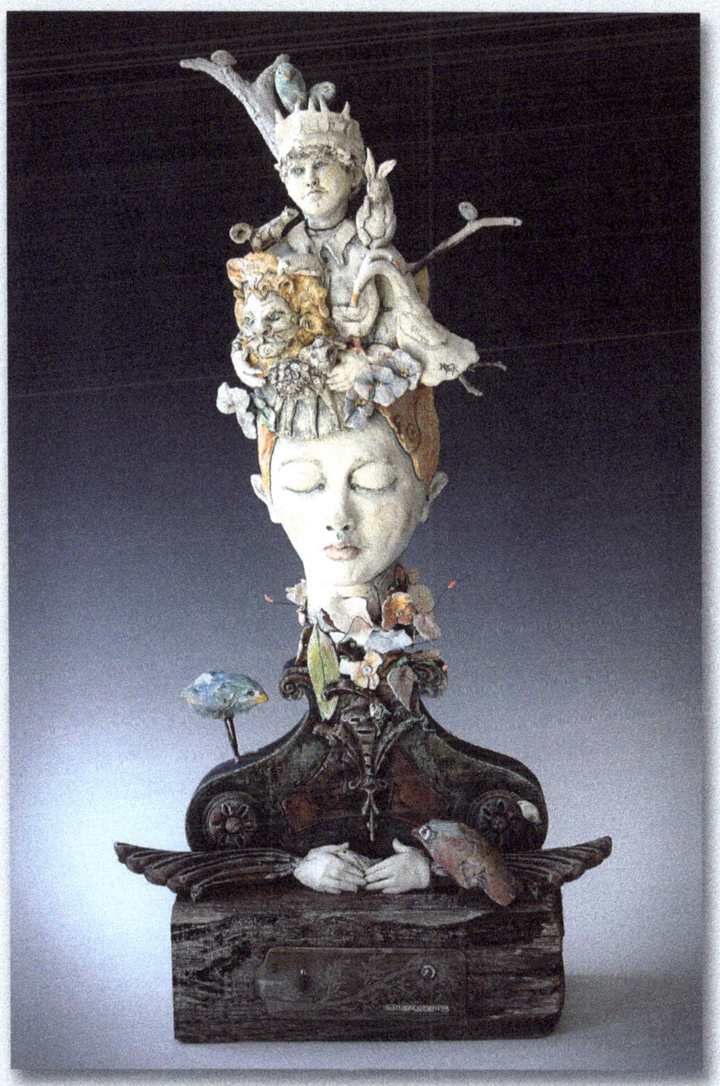

michelle tock york

goose girl's realm

clay & found object assemblage
29" x 16" x 6"

Goose Girl's Realm is derived from a Grimm's Fairy Tale where there is hope and a moral to the story. A place where a Utopian Society might exist in our imaginings and man, beast, woman and child live together in harmony. Yet, darkness lurks in the fringes of the illustrated images, the cracks in the clay, and in the narrative —much like real life.

Jake Sands

4 O'Clock in the Afternoon

Whenever he woke, he did not open his eyes until sometime after. This wasn't done out of reflex, but of a necessity. He had convinced himself that the day did not start until his eyes were open, nor did his dreams discharge after the rheum was removed. The light would bind the two for a moment, but there was no special hurry. He kept his thin lids shut for as long as he could stand it, wanting to remain immune to the charms of reality.

The sound of a blue jay is what usually made him get out of bed, and it made him miss the songs of the bluebirds, perched satisfied high in the birch trees of the islands to the north At first, he rose when this sound became too persistent, always tricking him into thinking it was early. Soon, he came to realize these birds and their sour squawking came at any hour of the day and with equal persistence. He stared out the shaded window, the bottom of its frame revealing dry and curling bits of red paint where the edges of the cheap blinds had been broken, the sun pouring its bright indifference on anything it could reach.

He stared out through the bright cracks of light and cursed the jays. The first few mornings they met his sight he appreciated their stark geometric tone, hoping their song was a histrionic gesture to their specific color and shape. Now, they sounded to him like a whimpering dog, the black angled streak around the neck choking whatever true song they were supposed to make.

A faint hiss from the southern road seemed to grow louder, He forced himself out of bed and opened the blinds, the sun drying whatever wet promise of the dream was left. There was no need to look, no reason to anticipate a prow of undulating dust; no reason to anticipate a visitor that he didn't want anyway. There had not been a car on this peninsula since last summer.

He used to walk down the road in the morning, the real morning, to town to get coffee and brandy before she came home from work. He never liked to be home when she arrived. He would sit up the road past the library and stare into the languid stream and watch the the sky moving, changing shape now and again from the soft urging of the clouds. He watched the eddies become arced with sterling as the sun came to them. He stared at the swirling forges until a sharp ache persisted, not bothering to blink. The stream was cold year round, but he never put his feet in after the long walk. He did not want to disturb the waters and the living things in it.

He knew she was home as he came up the road. The bottoms of the silver maples coated with new dust that concealed the ebullient dew. He felt like turning back into town. They had not been together for over a week. She opted to stay in town in the small concrete bunker next to the infirmary, not wanting to make the drive after her twelve-hour shifts. Besides, she always blamed him for her starched uniform getting dingy from the dust that came up from the road and blew in small amounts through the bedroom windows along the little flags that hung on the outside of the sil and would always roll up and hover from the wind in the soft, first light, when he did not know if he was asleep or awake. He lay there with his back away from her but feeling her shift in agreement with the first light, and it was in those hours they did all the communicating they needed to do. He always liked sleeping with the window open. He liked when he could sleep.

The kitchen was still damp and cool, even at this time of day. He made his way through the kitchen as bits of onion skin and garlic peels and egg shells stuck to his heels, He did not bother to remove them. The door to the mudroom was still open, with its broken bottom pane and with its strike plate bent and marred, one screw missing and most of the copper finish worn away. It's always hotter than you think, he thought as he stepped out on to the sunken concrete steps. His forehead instantly perspired and the sun caught it. He could see where the pollen had made soft inroads on the shed and picnic table in the yard, reminding him of the way it would stick to the wool of the few sheep they used to own and they would laugh but

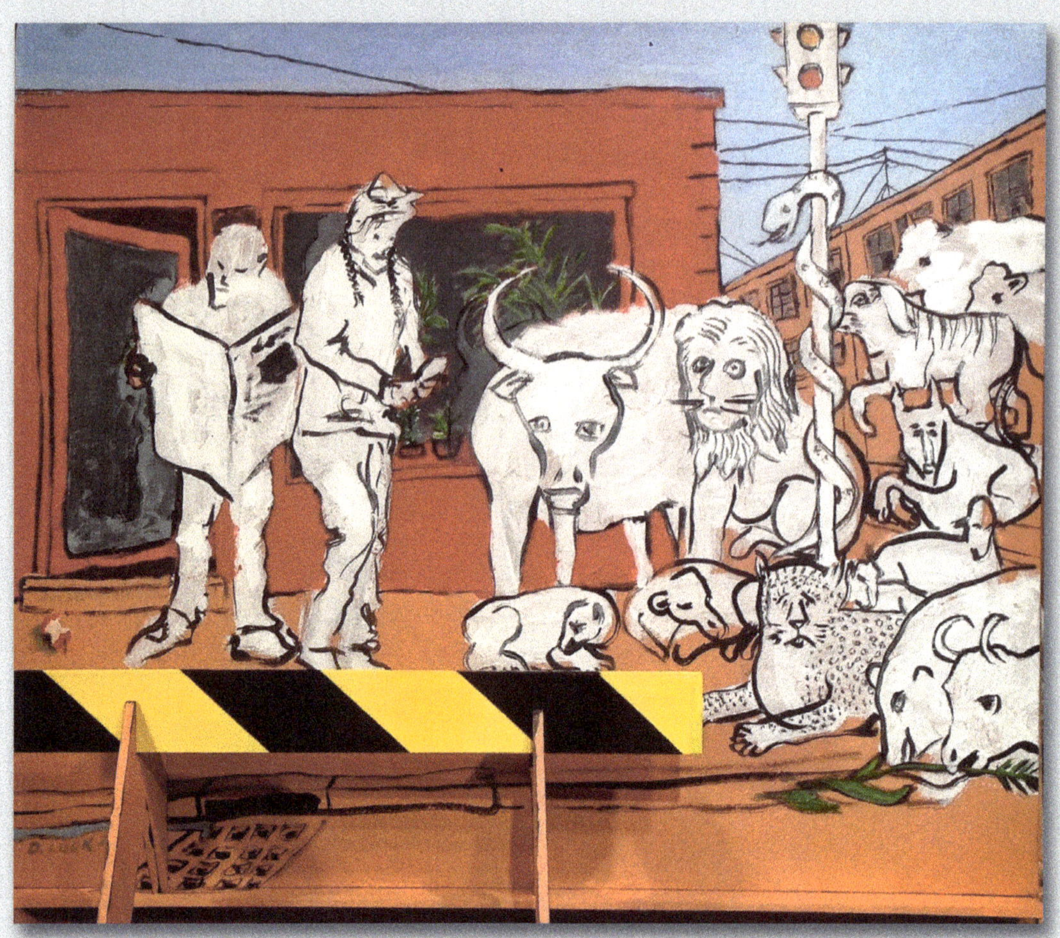

dan lisuk

peaceable neighborhood

acrylic on canvas
20″ X 24″

In this allegorical riff on Hicks' painting, time has advanced at the site of the former peaceable kingdom. Are these the ghosts of the past residents looking over the changes? The humans take advantage of new technology and wonder if communication has really improved. Is the florist's shop what's left of the Garden of Eden? Perhaps the apple core in front of the open door gives a clue. The Serpent watches the scene cunningly, perched on a pole whose light has no green. We look at the scene across a physical barrier. Some of the animals peer back at us, wondering. Others sleep or carry on their lives in blissful ignorance as best they can.

he thought it looked like a fungus, green and yellow and fuzzy. He could see small bits of it sticking to his arm and chest hair, though there was no wind to urge it. He could feel two rivulets of sweat moving from his armpits down to the top of his shorts. Hip wiped them away with the inside of his bicep, making a smear of older sweat and soil. He made his way under the silver maple and tried to relax, staring through the shade of the broad leaves as soft, dappled light dangled down. The shade cooled his brow and made him shiver imperceptible but he was still hot. The path down to the small lake was well overgrown and for a moment he could not remember which side the dock was on. It had to be east, he thought.

She never wanted to watch the sunrise. She was always late because of him. Awake before both her and the sun, he would idly thumb the dimple of dark hair at the small of her back that never showed when she was wearing her bathing suit; the pink suit never fit her quite well enough and never looked comforting against her dark skin, especially so late in the season. Her bottom was always full of some water as when she climbed onto the dock and the pinch from the clasp on her back remained well into the evening.

But he always liked to watch her swim, from one lazy, open eye while he lay on the dock, opting for sun rather than exercise, and always preferring to swim alone. The skin always looked whiter in the water as she kicked slowly to the bottom, the last he could see of her was the two bowling pin calves floating down, pushing the surface away, but then rising immediately as the water became to cold. She never had much grace to her stroke, though her too-broad shoulders carried her with ease the few hundred yards across the lake. She never went all the way to the opposite shore, just out of the sun and covered with a thin layer of algae. It made her nervous.

All but one edge of the dock he built was visible. He made the dock without any extravagance but with great precision and just big enough for two to sit on. The cheap metal pylons near the shore were sunken. The last one gathered the algae that the water lapped against it. The dock was rough underfoot, weatherbeaten and unused, yet shown argent against the lake from up the path. Small heads of rusted nails rose above sunken planks where the rain pooled on them. He thought about jumping in: there was something about the sapphire color that was inviting and comforting and maybe transforming, if he allowed himself to think that way. He stared at the lake a while longer until its edges were gone and the ache returned from the reflection of the sun. He blinked and looked back at the house. The silver maple hovered in front of the house and his window. He watched the tops of the tree sway silently, a quiet benediction as an act of service. He didn't wait for the wind to come to him, and walked quickly back to the house.

HIs eyes were closed, but he couldn't be sure if he had slept or not. His brow was tight from trying to force them to close. Or maybe it was from the sun from earlier. Or from not sleeping. He could not recall a time where he didn't feel the tight strain. He could taste the pollen in the corners of his mouth and felt the dried sweat on his brow as he tried to force himself to relax. The soft, laser echoing of the birched bluebirds in his mind now replaced by the dour, defeated songs outside.

So, this is how it happens, he thought. This is where it lives and won't leave again. It does not matter it you walk to town or open the window or become a bird or a sheep. It comes in the room, under the door but not the not the window, ignominious, creeping, with the same color and consistency of wet gravel. Shame comes at four o'clock in the afternoon when the sun is still out and it's too early to try and go back to sleep. It comes from laying in bed thinking of what you could've done with the day, and you use that time instead telling yourself that the night will be no better. The night is nothing, anyways. Bright sun and birdsongs do not always mean the day owes you anything and things will and do end in ruin when the earth is peaceful and quiet, just as the night is never a silky reprieve. The night always lies to you just as the day does. The promise that either brings is just an ill-fitting daydream, anyway. This is not a place to rest anymore, and you can't rest anyways, so what's the use? He turned away, both from the window and the door and brought his knees as close to this chest as he could. He closed his eyes as a reflex to being awake.

■

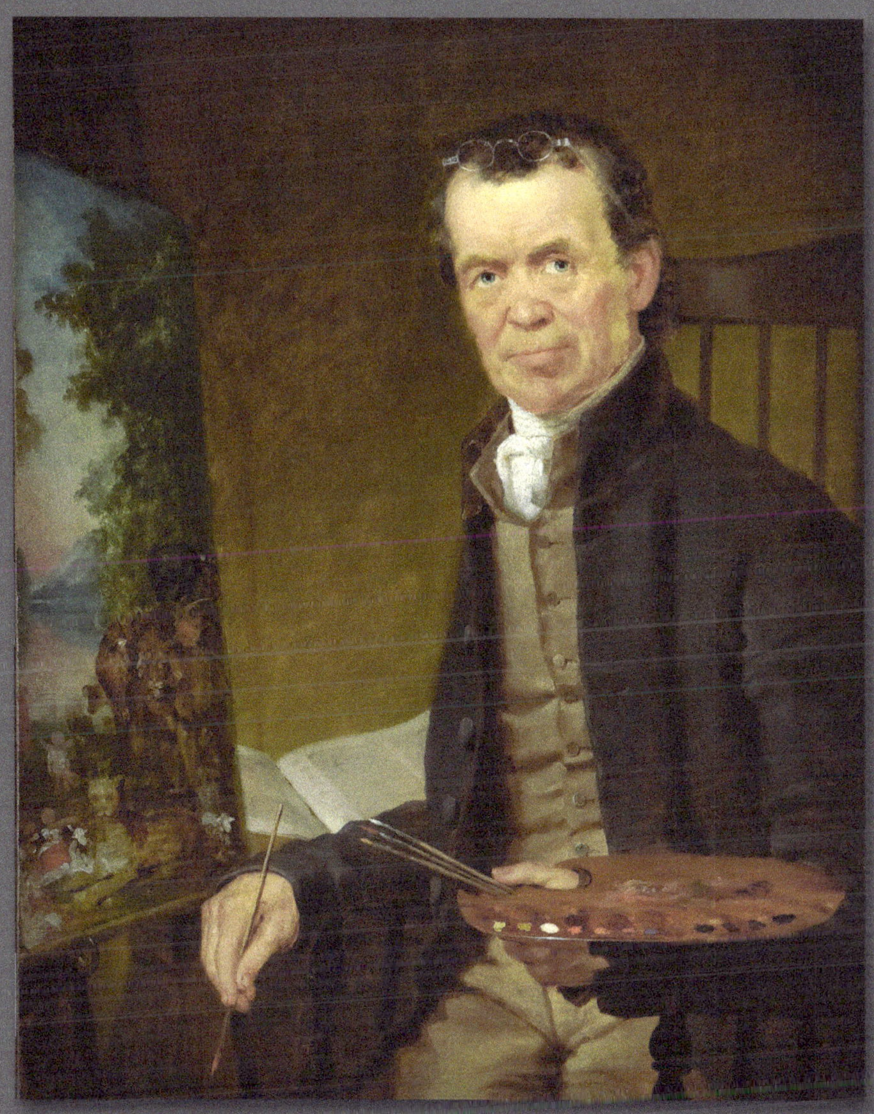

thomas hicks
portrait of edward hicks

ca. 1850-1852

James A. Michener Art Museum
Doylestown, Pennsylvania

Jennifer Yeatts

Peaceable Kingdom

If you aren't sure what to do when the river
Runs low, or if you still have to ask mother cheetah
When the rains will come, and in any case when your left

Arm is constantly reaching farther than your right
(Which feels prodigal somehow, in its own way),
Then little brother I say to you

with all the haughty sureness I can muster:
I know you want to run. I understand the impulse
Towards a giant leap across that canyon

Even though its chasm promises you only mystery
And mystery surely means pain. And pain, brother,
Pain isn't worth the risk. Stay here, young one,

Stay among the scolding eyes and curious deadly jawlines,
Stay a branch's length from the bear with the unfathomable snout,
For while her coat is sleek and black as the canyon,

While her jaw may snap in your direction any moment,
Still here between her hot torso and her fierce grip
She too carries a wounded heart, like me, like you.

And the calf at her shoulder bleats trust.
And the corn in her teeth will feed us.

You are strong for your size and determined.
You are willful, not likely to hear.
Your foothold will slip and my fingertips

Will miss gripping your yellow curls.
Our uncle, on the river's far bank, will forget
there were three, will squint briefly,

will move us along to the next treaty site.
Our makers, our kingdom,
Won't follow.

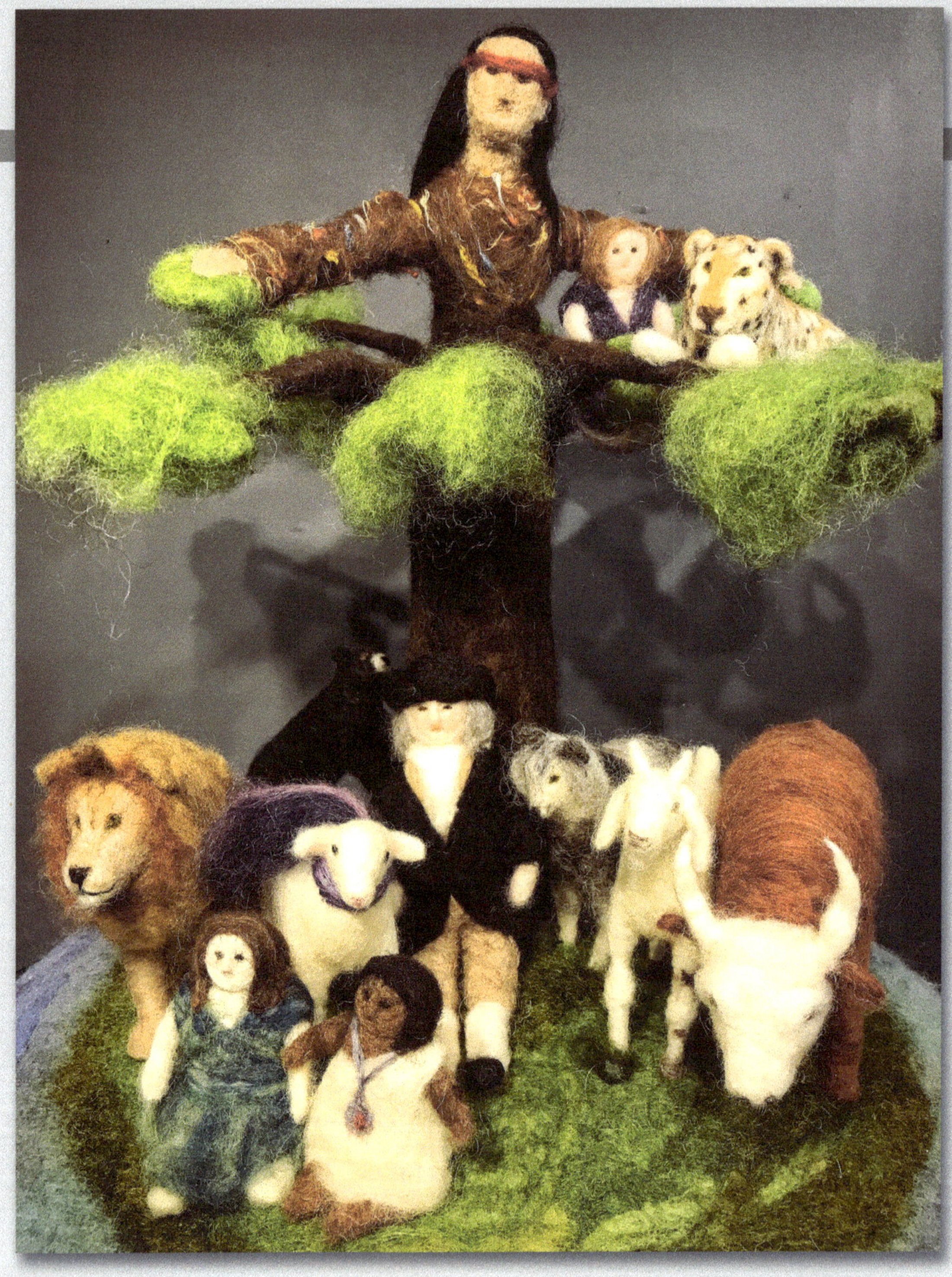

sarah tierney

rising waters, back to the future

fine art/needle & wet felted
21″ x 28″

Rising Waters, Back to the Future, my channeling of Edward Hicks' *Peaceable Kingdom*. My work was created by hand needle felting and wet felting wool, Alpaca and some mohair fibers. The animals, children, William Penn and Native American tree are 3-D and sculpted using one barbed needle to interlock the natural fibers. The base is a layering of approximately eight or more layers of fiber, needle felted then wet felted. I used some wire armature for the standing animals and tree then felted the wool with the barbed needle as I created the sculpture.

My inspiration for this piece was based on William Penn's treaty with the Native Americans, the Native Americans being one with nature. Sadly, the broken treaties by future settlers and subsequent decline of our environment, therefore falling short of being good stewards of God's creation. The rising water is from climate change endangering humans and animals. I wanted to depict that animals, both herbivores and carnivores and humans are all on an island facing the same fate. Edward Hicks and his seeming spiritual connection to animals touched me because I care deeply for animals and their welfare so it became a wonderful challenge to not only interpret Edward Hicks' work but create a work of love from my connection with spirituality, animals and nature.

Anne-Marie Oomen

Sixty Plus Versions

> The carnivorous beasts—lions, leopards, wolves—grow in size. Where once they had cast their eyes docilely to the ground, they now stare out, alert, aggressive, challenging, even rabidly agitated.
>
> — Holland Cotter, "Finding Endless Conflict Hidden in a Peaceable Kingdom," *The New York Times*, June 16, 2000

Always, the Inner Light forked,
split the landscape, faulted it.
You won't see that   at first.

The ox settles peaceably
near the lion, but look closely: despite
muzzles nuzzling straw, not   at ease.

In later versions the lion's eyes
enlarge, look straight at the painter,
at me,   sear our   futures

toward some tainted history, smoked, mirrored,
the murder of the innocents' innocence
guised as   defense.

The lion knows this, as does
lumbering ox at his straw, the tiger,
goats, leopards,   even lambs—

all but the child, dressed in white,
always in veils   of that inner light.
Sixty times Edward gathered   them,

set them on the brink.
They face the edge, again abyss.
Dose paradise   come   to this?

How many times does the lion
stare me down? How many times the child
misses falling to the gorge?   Until

at last Penn's treaty flutters
in the canvas corner,
composition decomposing   betrayal.

In final versions, Edward tired the lion,
eyes strained with seeing;
stilling time,   distilling

morning, noon, twilight's inner
light, that one hour when
the kingdom   might have been,
the child come safely   among the men.

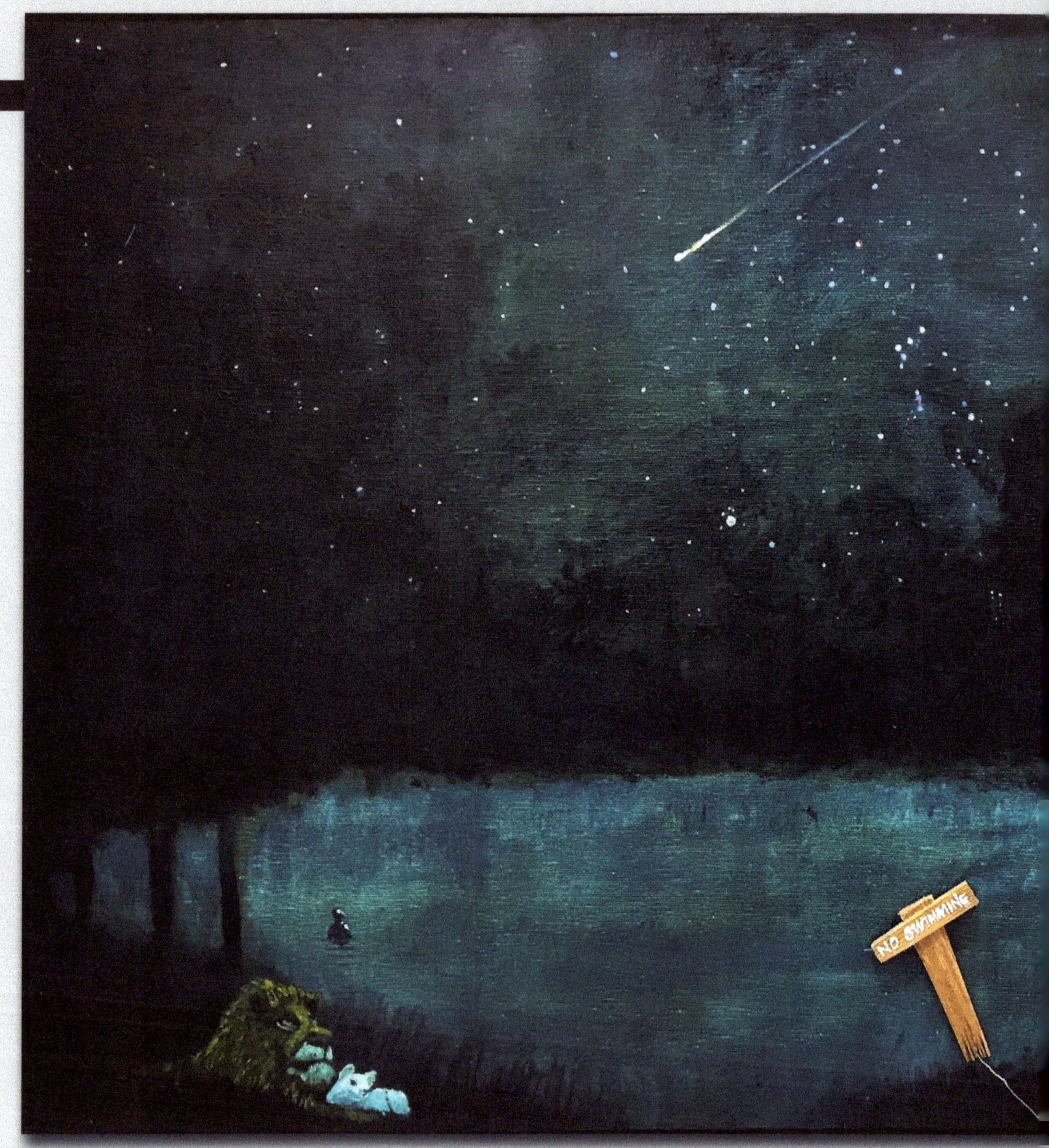
NO SWIMMING

greg nachazel
i'm still searching

oil
24 x 30″

It is such an overwhelming joy to be asked in the form of an intelligent assignment to create something of value in two dimensions and be awarded six months of time to prepare. Being allowed to think about it, if one is serious, provides for a thoughtful work. Fine Art, if it is fine, captures the eye and contains meaningful values that transcend mere singularity of form. Content and Substance while delicately and thoughtfully woven into a composition provide for all manner of intellectual and emotional adventure. The depth of this adventure falls entirely upon the person standing in front of the artwork.

Many people are comfortable on shore and satisfied to just sit and let life blow over them like rows of dunegrass. Other people swim out, dive deep, and occasionally return to land clinging to the dripping wet treasure left behind by souls once on the water, lost in the grips of nature from another time. Dive in and swim in this midnight river, maybe it is all that remains of a dream; a Peaceable Kingdom. Isaiah was inspired and "painted" his picture in words 2760 years ago. This painting is only a few months old.

CONTRIBUTING WRITERS

ALISON ARTHUR

living arts guide
dipping my toes and more in various art forms
yoga, cooking, writing, painting, gardening, music making, swimming
guiding others in a few
always a student, sometimes instructing

ROBB ASTOR grew up along Lake Michigan in the village of Pentwater. He served as a Peace Corps Volunteer in the United Republic of Tanzania. Robb lives in Traverse City, Michigan. His collection of poetry, *Bitter Dagaa*, was selected for publication by Michigan Writers Cooperative Press in 2014. A number of his poems have been published in the *Dunes Review*. Many things inform Robb's poetry— the natural spaces of Northern Michigan, astronomy, but mostly the daily wonder of encountering beauty in the strangest of things.

LUISE BOLLEBER received her Creative Nonfiction Writing MFA from Lesley University in Cambridge, Massachusetts in 2009. She lives in Traverse City, Michigan.

FLEDA BROWN's *The Woods Are On Fire: New & Selected Poems*, was chosen by Ted Kooser for his University of Nebraska poetry series in 2017. She has nine previous collections of poems. Her work has twice appeared in *The Best American Poetry* and has won a Pushcart Prize, the Felix Pollak Prize, the Philip Levine Prize, and the Great Lakes Colleges New Writer's Award, and has twice been a finalist for the National Poetry Series. She was poet laureate of Delaware from 2001-07. She now lives with her husband, Jerry Beasley, in Traverse City and is on the faculty of the Rainier Writing Workshop, a low-residency MFA program in Tacoma, Washington.

MARINA CALL is a travel writer and educator, and author of the novel *Eastbound, I Think*. She has a slight obsession with trains, food and words.

BETSY EMDIN has a MFA in Creative Nonfiction from Goucher College. A chapter of her thesis was the basis for a segment on *This American Life*. She's also had short essays in *The New York Times*, *The Sun*, *The Christian Science Monitor*, and *Midwest Living*. She grew-up in Grand Rapids, raised her family in Holland, MI, and has lived in Traverse City for ten years where she works as a house manager at the State and Bijou theaters.

ALICE HANSEN lives in Traverse City and spends every other Saturday with her writing group. Her "Symphony" was her reaction to the Edward Hicks painting during a 10-minute timed writing in a group session.

BRIAN COLE ILER is from the metro Detroit area, and moved to the Grand Traverse region in 2012. He is an abstract visual art maker who ventured into the theater realm in 2013. As of late 2017 he has been writing short plays and vignettes, mostly for a new company called Theatre Rogue. Usually it works vice-versa, but Brian has found that words can often express ideas in a way that painting or drawing cannot. Who'd have thunk it?!

PAUL MAXBAUER is a retired history teacher living in Traverse City. He spends his time reading, writing and enjoying outdoor activities.

ELAINE MCINTOSH is a retired nurse practitioner trying to live peaceably with the bears, foxes, owls living in the woods with her in Fife Lake ,Michigan. She has had her poems published in *Huron River Review, Dunes Review,* and *Bear River Review*.

The Rev. **ROBERT MCQUILKIN**, graduate of the College of Wooster and McCormick Theological Seminary, served four churches over his 40 year career as a Presbyterian pastor.

SPENCER NYE will be a senior at Frankfort High School in Benzie County, Michigan.

SUSAN ODGERS, an honored psychology instructor at NMC for the past thirty years, is a member of several area boards and councils. Since 2008, she's written a column for the *Traverse City Record-Eagle*. A 2017 Ragdale Fellow, she's the vice president of Michigan Writers and co-hosts the monthly series "Poets Meet Musicians."

ANNE-MARIE OOMEN is author of *The Lake Michigan Mermaid* with Linda Nemec Foster; *Love, Sex and 4-H* (Next Generation Indie Award for Memoir); *Pulling Down the Barn* (Michigan Notable Book); and *Uncoded Woman* (poetry), among others. She teaches at Solstice MFA at Pine Manor College (MA), Interlochen's College of Creative Arts (MI), and at conferences throughout the country.

After more than four decades teaching writing at Northwestern Michigan College, **JOHN PAHL** is now somewhat retired, staying active by helping to raise a teen-aged daughter and participating in a local creative writing group, as well as teaching part time for Ferris State University. He works as a freelance editor for Mission Point Press and occasionally writes copy for local non-profits. His publications over the years include poems in *Vallum Magazine* (Montreal), *Dunes Review, Parallel 45, Pine Cone Review,* and stories and articles in *The Funnel* (Fulbright journal), *NISOd's Innovation Abstracts* and for The Commission on Higher Education. He enjoys stream fishing for trout and sailing on Grand Traverse Bay.

ELIZABETH PAXSON is a visual artist and poet/writer. She is a graduate of the Interlochen Arts Academy and the Minneapolis College of Art and Design. Her work has appeared in journals and other publications, and she has shown and sold her art in Michigan, Maine, Boston and Chicago. Her first chapbook of poems will be published this year with Redbird Chapbooks of St. Paul, Minnesota.

JOANNA PEPE: One Saturday morning in early May, our women's writing group "Nudge" chose Hicks's *Peaceable Kingdom painting as a writing prompt. Sitting in my living room, surrounded by a wil*d and wooded fairyland of evergreens and maples, the photocopied painting took center stage. To my delight I was transported to Italy, *where "La Donna* Guarda Negli Occhi *del Leone" paid me a visit.*

A native of Flint, Michigan, **JAKE SANDS** spent the last 10 years exploring the country, with stints in Portland, Oregon; Spearfish, South Dakota; Chattanooga, Tennessee; and the Red River Gorge of Kentucky. He is an avid rock climber and a student of the human condition. Having recently relocated to Traverse City, he hopes to draw inspiration from the area and start work on his first novel.

JENNIFER SPERRY STEINORTH is a poet, educator, collaborative artist, and licensed builder living in northern Michigan. Her poetry has appeared in *Alaska Quarterly, Beloit Poetry Journal, The Colorado Review, FourWayReview, The Journal, jubilat, Michigan Quarterly Review, Mid-American Review, Poetry Northwest, Sixth Finch, Quarterly West* and elsewhere. She has received grants from the Sewanee Writers Conference, The Vermont Studio Center,

Warren Wilson College whence an MFA in poetry, and The Bear River Writers Conference. In 2016 she was the Writers@Work Poetry Fellow and won The Connecticut River Review Poetry Prize.

DANIEL STEWART is a writer and storyteller, as well as a writing coach and book designer through his consultancy, History By Design. He holds a PhD in history and writes memoir, personal essay and fiction. His work has appeared in academic and literary journals, and he is currently completing a memoir and a novel. He is a past president of Michigan Writers and lives on an old farmstead in Leelanau County with his wife and a number of animals, some of them invited.

PATRICIA TRENTACOSTE is a retired philosophy instructor (Oakland University and Wayne State), now living in northern Michigan. Past publications include essays in academic journals, a true-life piece for *Woman's Day Magazine*, and a bi-weekly feature column for *The Voice* (Macomb and St. Clair Counties). Her recent fiction has appeared in *Dunes Review* and *Adelaide Literary Journal*. She currently serves on the board of Michigan Writers, Inc. She also makes kinetic Nature-mobiles and volunteers as an art and writing mentor for the Benzie County Juvenile Court system.

CATHERINE TURNBULL's poems have appeared in *Tupelo Quarterly*, *Dos Passos Review*, *The Green Mountains Review*, *Dunes Review*, and others. In 2008, a chapbook, *The Chocolatier Speaks of His Wife*, was published by MI Writers Cooperative Press. A manuscript in progress, *The Spider's Apprentice*, was a finalist for the Tupelo Press Dorset Prize in 2015 and 2016.

JENNIFER YEATTS' work has previously appeared in a few places here and there, though not so much recently. She received her MFA from the University of Idaho and currently writes from Traverse City, Michigan, where she is director of coffee at Higher Grounds Trading Company.

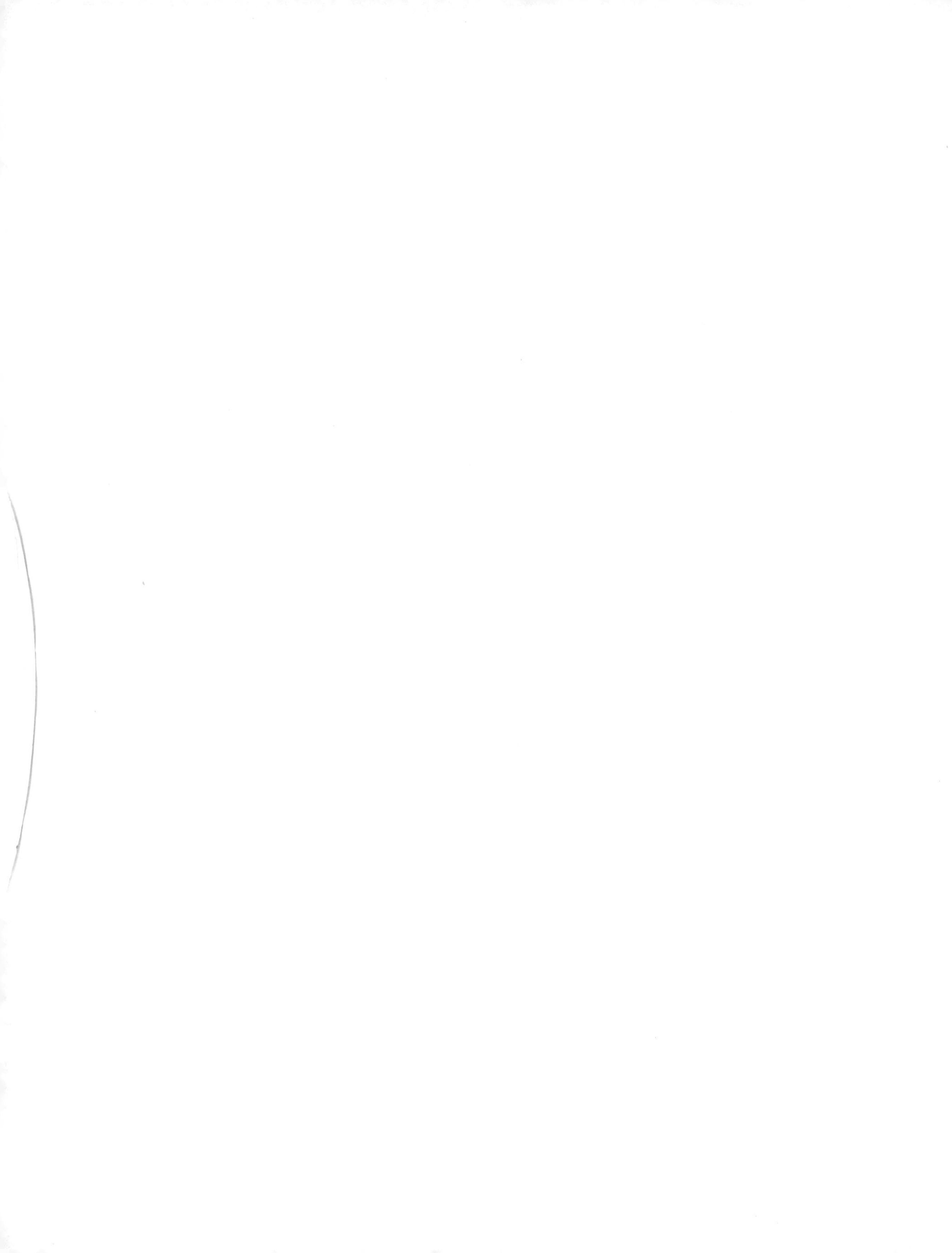

www.ingramcontent.com/pod-product-compliance
Lightning Source LLC
Chambersburg PA
CBHW042046030726
47599CB00019B/2382

* 9 7 8 1 9 4 9 2 8 5 0 0 0 *